Travels and Adventures of an Orchid Hunter

Travels and Adventures of an Orchid Hunter

An Account of Canoe and Camp Life in Colombia While Collecting Orchids in the Northern Andes

Albert Millican

Copyright

Contents

CHAPTER I

HAVING FULLY MADE UP my mind for a long sea voyage, and taken my ticket for anywhere and everywhere beyond the seas, I provided myself with a stock of knives, cutlasses, revolvers, rifle, an overflowing supply of tobacco and newspapers, and started on the third Saturday of the eighth month of Her Majesty Queen Victoria's Jubilee year. After the usual ceremony of tipping railway porters and cabdrivers I went on board the steam-tug *Sunshine*, taking passengers and mails from the Princess Landing Stage, Liverpool, for embarkation on the Celestial Company's steamship *Phantom*, then bound for the Spanish Main. A few minutes' sail brought us alongside the *Phantom*, where after a careful inspection of the eating saloon, cabins, water filters, etc., by my unhappy relatives, who consisted of several maiden aunts, fifth cousins, and godchildren, they eventually said "Good-bye," and, as if to drive home the old-fashioned words, each gave me at parting a remorseless hug.

No sooner had the *Sunshine* re-embarked her living freight of weeping relatives, overgrown ships' agents, and postmen, than a shrill screech from the funnel of the *Sunshine*, echoed back by a dull crunching sound from the screw of the *Phantom*, announced to all on board that we were in a fair way for a separation for an indefinite period from wives and sweethearts, as well as the soothing associations of an English fireside.

The *Phantom*, although only a small ship of 200 tons burden, soon showed her superiority of sailing over her other river companions by passing many large ships, which seemed to me to be encumbered by a superfluous arrangement of poles and white cotton; and it was not long before the white-crested rollers of the ocean showed us that the mudbanks of the Mersey were left far behind.

On looking round for what society the ship afforded I found Spratt, the captain, an excellent fellow, who, besides the valuable information acquired by a long experience in and out of almost every port on the surface of the globe, possessed a good vein of humor—not at all despisable under the circumstances. Besides, he was not given to boring his companions in conversation with a long history of how many of those remarkable beings called lords, earls, dukes, marquesses, etc., he had safely piloted over the Atlantic. I also noticed two of the passengers: the one a stout, burly gentleman, of from forty-five to fifty years of age, to all appearances a retired sea captain (it might have been of a slave-trader); the other a delicate lady of eighteen—a beauty with the figure of a Venus and the features of a nymph, and a pair of large, black fathomless eyes that would grace an Andalusian, whose melancholy was softened by dimpled cheeks of the most delicate peach-bloom, the whole framed with a rich profusion of waving raven hair, a glance at which was sufficient to give you the impression that you had the pleasure of seeing a beautiful woman. A casual observer would imagine that the relationship between the elderly gentleman and the fair young lady was that of father and daughter, or guardian and ward. Imagine my surprise when at lunchtime I heard bald-headed Mr. Sharpies inquire, "Can I help you to a little of this fish, Mrs. Sharpies?" As I looked across the table I thought I detected a slight shrug of the fair shoulders, and the melancholy of the melancholy eyes intensify. There might be something of sorrow hid behind so extraordinary a union! However, all the explanation that ever I had was contained in the underside of the lid of a workbasket, where, accidentally, I saw stitched, in letters of comfort, "Better be an old man's darling than a young man's slave."

As we steamed slowly away from land each one on board seemed to linger on deck to watch the grey line of cliffs grow fainter and more undistinguishable until finally nothing was left to us of Old England but cherished recollections—and night throwing her dusky mantle over all, those who could began to seek asylum in their cabins, glad to escape from the weariness of a long day's excitement, the beautiful calm of the sea reassuring even the most timid. And now, for the benefit of those who are not accustomed to ship's bedroom furniture, let me endeavour to describe that in use on the *Phantom*. The bedsteads, commonly dubbed with the unceremonious titles of bunks, are really large shelves, two in each room, one placed above the other; the lower one about two feet from the floor and the other about four feet, very much reminding one of the shelves used in larders for jam, etc., except that each shelf is provided with a high edge, being a board about a foot and a half wide; this, with the four-feet distance from the floor, renders it absolutely indispensable for the occupant of the top shelf to perform night and morning, or as often as required, a no very desirable feat of gymnastics in order to place himself behind the side of the shelf.

Apart from this stiffness in the bedsteads, everything seemed to be made on an opposite principle, water bottles, candlesticks, towel-rails, etc., being suspended with as many joints as would lead one to imagine that each had emanated from a school of engineering where the application of the ball-and-socket was a speciality. However, after the foregoing inventory of my bedroom furniture and a marvelous triumph of agility that I really never gave myself credit for, I managed to scramble safely on to one of the shelves, the lower one, as may be supposed, where, after some dim visions of shipwreck, pirates, and cannibal islands, I slept soundly until six o'clock next morning, and I was only awakened by an extraordinary motion alternately elevating my head and heels above the level of my body.

Hastily dressing and going on deck, I found that through the night a strong headwind had arisen, whipping the sea into large foam-crested rolling billows and making our little *Phantom* swing and dance in a way that would put a switchback railway in the shade. One side of the ship would suddenly dive down until the top of her deck touched the water, while the other side was high in the air at an elevation of thirty feet, and this, in turn, would descend with a splash and a roar; at the same time several tons of salt water would sweep across her upper decks, and as quickly, with the change of position, blow over the side, this continual vibration being kept up for a period of not less than four days and four nights, sufficient to convince nervous people not accustomed to seafaring peculiarities that the owners of the Phantom had secretly entered into a contract with the society for the development of the theory of perpetual motion. This unwarrantable infringement of the commonest laws of equilibrium materially affected the comfortable enjoyment of a bill of fare which, although really good for the situation, was not absolutely free from that inevitable repetition of certain dishes to commemorate days of the week. For instance, pea soup Wednesdays and Fridays, plum dough Sundays and Thursdays, a regularity strangely peculiar to gaols, workhouses, and barracks, and a system by which sailors mark the days of the week without the assistance of Whitaker.

The table was provided with two long laths, which extended the whole length of each side at a sufficient distance from each other to admit of a plate being firmly wedged between the two, leaving room at the corners for all indispensable table utensils. The dishes containing the food were arranged in a line along the middle of the table, each dish partitioned off from his neighbour by a capacious bolster of serviettes; but even this contrivance did not prevent the chicken from dexterously changing places with the sardines, or the butter becoming irretrievably mixed with the curry, in a way which, even considering the extraordinary motion of the ship, appeared perfectly ludicrous. An attempt to avoid an overbalance by clutching your chair with both hands (which chair, by the way, is screwed securely to the floor) would result in the upsetting of a cup of hot coffee into your lap, or the inundation of your plate by the contents of an adjoining water bottle.

On retiring to my cabin in the evening, I was greeted from the surrounding partitions with most unearthly sounds of choking. On inquiry, I was informed that all the ladies on board had been attacked with that uncomfortable disorder of the nerves or stomach called seasickness, which effectually confined them to their cabins for the ensuing week. And now how to sleep in a bedroom performing such extraordinary antics was a problem not easily solved. It occurred to me to imitate the fellow who, on account of the effects of an overdose of Pommery '76, or some more disreputable stuff, sat down on the floor to wait until the bedstead would stop for him to get into bed. However, after this experience, the rude wind finally betook himself to other climes to play his unwelcome pranks, and the sea settled down from a turbulent, boiling mass of white foam to that calm, placid blue, that would fain make believe it was always like that.

All this time we had seen nothing but an occasional passing ship of the kind I had remarked coming out of the Mersey, so superfluously encumbered with sticks and cords. Now their utility became apparent: each bundle of cloth had been unwound and dexterously hung in a position best calculated to court the society of the fickle breeze; each available corner was crowded, and the spotless whiteness of the canvas—intensified by the bright sunlight and the soft blue of the ocean—when contrasted with our own combination of smoky funnels and clanking engines, would drive one to imagine that the strange fantastic craft was a visitor from the supernatural, or that Mercury, to better perform some peculiar nautical errand, had taken upon him the form of a gigantic sea-bird. However, putting all allegory aside, there is no more beautiful sight at sea than a full-rigged ship in sail on a fine day.

After about six days' sailing I noticed one morning a long dark-grey line on the horizon, which I imagined in my want of marine experience to be some passing whale—or, better still, could it not be the long-chronicled and much-exaggerated sea-serpent out for his morning gambol? This pleasing delusion was quickly dispelled when Captain Spratt politely informed me that my wonderful sea-serpent was nothing less than the island called Terceira, one of the Azores, situated in Lat. 38 deg. 37 min. N., and Long. 27 deg. 13 min. W., furnishing a beautiful semi-tropical retreat for visitors, and a most useful coaling-station in any emergency for vessels crossing the Atlantic.

The *Phantom* kept on her course, making for the West Indian island of Barbados. The passengers passed the time lounging on deck, smoking, and watching the large flights of flying-fish which rose out of the water at intervals and skimmed along a distance of thirty yards, making their large wing-like fins glisten in the sunshine like burnished silver, and then dipped themselves again into the water to be refreshed after so extraordinary an exertion. Those who have been long out at sea in fine weather cannot fail to remark the gorgeous spectacle presented by a sunset in a tropical latitude. As the mighty orb sinks slowly behind the distant band of blue, large masses of milky clouds gather around to honor the departure of the king of day, and in return for it we passed the fine barracks, the shrill bugle call reminded us of the company of British officers and men who were passing a lively time amongst the agreeable Barbadians, and who, from what stray political opinions I could overhear, appeared quite able to set us an example in loyalty. The *Phantom* took up her position amongst the many other ships which were engaged in discharging cargo, or awaiting orders from England.

The houses of Bridgetown fringing the harbor are constructed of a light pinky stone, which, seen in the strong light of this climate, presents a most attractive appearance. Almost before the anchors had swung out of the bows of the *Phantom*, the ship was surrounded by a crowd of curly-pated negroes, with long rows of white teeth and rolling eyes contrasting amusingly with their ebony features. Some would make dexterous plunges and come up again on the other side of the ship, performing the clever feat for sixpence, while a group of youngsters were fighting and sputtering for occasional pence thrown to them by the passengers. Others would display a collection of wares for sale, all expressing their opinion or courting attention in a kind of jargon which reduced the Queen's English to a most miserable snarl.

After the usual visit of inspection from doctors and custom-house officers, we were at liberty to go ashore—by the medium of one of the many boats either hovering in the vicinity of the ship or crowding around the gangway, each of their black owners, meanwhile, squabbling for patronage. I need hardly say that all on board the *Phantom* who could, availed themselves of the positive luxury of a little exercise on terra firm after a fortnight's cramping in bunks and deck chairs. A few well-directed strokes brought us to shore, and no more extraordinary sight presented itself to the newly-arrived European than the motley medley of human faces, from the fair rose of the delicate European lady to the polished black of the negro, with the various between–shades, all busy about their morning marketing. The lover of tropical curios will find here quite a museum to choose from: pink and white coral of the most delicate shades, gossamer masterpieces of the coral insect's ingenuity, patterns worthy of imitation by our most skillful lace and filigree workers; midget hummingbirds in scarlet and green, which Nature—indulgent goddess! has provided with a special Court-dress to enable them more effectually to steal the virtue of innocent flowers; delicate leaves and blossoms cunningly manufactured from glittering fish-scales; work in seeds, moss, and tortoiseshell; in short, everything beautiful and curious, well calculated to draw the money out of foreigners' pockets. Passing through streets of well-kept shops, mostly uncomfortably crowded with groups of gossiping negroes, we finally arrived at the principal hotel, called the Ice House, where each thirsty soul indulged in ice cream or native lemonade, which was most refreshing considering the thermometer at this time registered the modest figure of 90 deg. Fahr. in the shade.

After an hour's stroll amongst the pretty villas, gardens, and plantations of the suburbs, the hoisting of the blue peter and the sound of a gun informed us that the *Phantom* was ready to continue the journey; so we lost no time in getting on board, and as we steamed slowly out of the harbor another glimpse at the beautiful surroundings extorted from us a sigh of regret at so short a stay, and a hope to return at no distant period.

CHAPTER II

THE *PHANTOM* QUICKLY GOT UNDERWAY, making for the island of Trinidad, and early next morning, as we turned up on deck, we were greeted by the peaks and undulations of the principal island; but as we are bound for the harbor and town of Port of Spain, we must pass through one or other of the four or live channels made by small islands lying between Trinidad and the mainland of Venezuela. Making every excuse for my deficiency in accurate geological information, it appears to me that the position of the islands would suggest to the most unobservant the idea that at some antediluvian or more remote period these colossal pyramids had formed part of the great continent of South America, and that, to satisfy one of Nature's capricious whims, they had been disconnected and arranged in their present picturesque situation. Be that as it may, as the little *Phantom* steamed gaily through one of the small openings between the islands the most unenthusiastic could not fail to be moved to admiration at the magnificent sight presented by the tremendous precipices rising to a thousand feet, almost perpendicularly. At not more than half a mile from the ship on each side were rugged peaks, ornamented at the top with straggling vegetation and tenanted by myriads of screaming seabirds, while the lower part was riddled by enormous subterranean caverns—once, perhaps, affording warehousing and apartments for enterprising pirates, now only a playground for the sportive waves which one after another resolve themselves into clouds of spray, with a wild murmuring sound, fit music for so romantic a situation. Passing further through the Strait, we caught a glimpse of the blackened hulk of what was once a fine sailing ship, carried on to the merciless rocks by the current which sweeps through between the various islands with great force. The vessel at the time of the disaster was laden with coolies, who were all happily rescued by a passing steamer.

Along the coast, between the Bocas and Port of Spain, the shore is interspersed and ornamented by many small bathing stations, owned by the more wealthy townspeople—pretty secluded retreats almost hidden by clumps of tangling vegetation; and, as if to break the wildness of the rugged, uninhabited hills, the passer-by is treated to a varying panorama of beautiful scenery furnished by a continuation of tiny islands, seven or eight in number, one larger than the rest furnishing accommodation for a commodious convict prison. By the aid of a field-glass, it is easy to distinguish long lines of unfortunates pacifying justice by arduous labour. Another of the larger islands is used as a coolie station, where the newly-imported East Indiamen find an asylum until their services are in demand for the sugar plantations. Half a dozen of the other islands are each about an acre in extent, all boasting spacious mansions and gardens and an enviable appearance of seclusion from prying eyes. Passing these smaller islands soon brought us in sight of the harbour, gay with ships from many nations. Several of the brightly painted paddle steamers which ply on the river Orinoco, at this time in the port, were almost enough to tempt a rambler to compromise himself for a trip. The usual formalities over, we were not long in getting ashore, to make ourselves as much acquainted with Trinidad as time would allow.

We found the streets and squares of the town very much wider and more commodious than those of Barbados. After strolling through the principal business thoroughfares, we were content to avail ourselves of a conveyance to make the circuit of the Savanna, about which we had heard so much; and I can assure any visitor not acquainted with these islands that to miss the opportunity would be a mistake. We found the Savanna nothing more than a large recreation ground of no extraordinary beauty, encircled by a carriage drive of some miles in length; but, excepting a large space occupied by the governor's house and gardens, almost the whole length of the route is enlivened by most exquisite little villas, built after good designs, painted in cheerful colors, and draped with a profusion of tropical plants, varying from the most delicate to the most extravagant tints. One is almost hidden by myriads of pale pink flowers of the *Bougainvillea glabra*. On another the white stars of the jasmine contrast with the rich blue of the ipomea. Another of these fairy little retreats is ornamented with splashing fountains and groups of palms, the rich green of which contrasts well with the bright patches of colour in the way of yellow crotons and scarlet poncianas, with other wonderful and beautiful collections of tropical plants whose long scientific names it would tire to enumerate. Whatever the spacious Government House may lack in beauty of architecture is amply made up for in profuse horticultural decorations. Besides smaller shrubs and climbers, there are magnificent clumps of tall feathery bamboos, curious banyans, and the remarkable *Strelitzia Reginae* with a perfect head of thirty feet in breadth. The day of our visit being a holiday, the young athletes of Trinidad were engaged in a cricketing contest with a neighboring island and the Savanna was gay with bunting, as well as pretty faces. We were very favorably impressed with the social character of the people of Trinidad, who seem to me to possess at once the stability of John Bull, combined with the elegance of the Spaniard and the politeness of the French. Visitors favored with more time than we were will, I have no doubt, agreeably prove what I say to be true. For my own part, when the usual sailing signal warned me that the *Phantom* was going in search of fresh sights, whether I accompanied or not, I was reluctant enough to leave so inviting and genial a place.

A few strong pulls brought us on board, and we were very quickly under weigh for the harbour of La Guayra, on the mainland of South America. The morning after leaving Trinidad we passed alongside the island of Margarita—a long, straggling, barren looking tract of land, which appeared to have little or no cultivation and few or no inhabitants, and at once associated with itself Robinson Crusoe-like adventures for anyone having ill luck enough to be cast on such an inhospitable-looking place. We were informed that at one time this was a pearl-fishing station, and at present there are some copper mines worked by European enterprise. Some two or three dozen natives, out in small canoes, engaged in fishing, hove near the ship as we were passing, in order to satisfy their curiosity on our no doubt novel appearance. Their boats were of the most primitive construction, seeming almost too frail to put to sea in. The men were of pure Indian race, a kind of dull brick colour, fine stalwart fellows, who seemed to despise fashion so much as almost to do without clothing altogether.

After forty-eight hours' sail we arrived in sight of the harbour of La Guayra, the principal port of Venezuela, which presents from the sea a magnificent panorama of scenery. A towering peak a mile and a quarter high seems to pierce the clouds. The almost perpendicular sides of the mountain bristle with large cacti, while around the foot the little town of La Guayra, from the brightness of the walls and tiling seen in the strong light of a tropical sun, presents a pleasing contrast with the dark grey and green of the mountain background. High up the hillside a small fort breaks the wildness of the situation, and, whatever may be its merits or defects from a defensive point of view, it certainly adds to the picturesqueness of the scene. A little lower down a large circus-like building is easily distinguishable, which we afterwards learn is the bull-fighting arena—without which no South American town of any pretensions would be considered complete. No sooner had the *Phantom* dropped anchor at a safe distance from the stormy coast than we were besieged as usual by an army of customhouse officers—who are especially officious at this place—and in their scrupulous anxiety to prevent the importation of anything approaching the character of contraband ammunition or infernal machines would scarcely pass a superfluous toothbrush or half-worn collar-box—disputing everything in a nasal, half intelligible Spanish, which sounds to an Englishman's ears unpleasantly like the action of a file on saw-teeth.

Landing at La Guayra for passengers is very difficult, and even dangerous, on account of a heavy swell rolling in from the sea and dashing in broken spray over the frail landing-stage, and more than likely giving the traveler a sound baptism of salt water. Once on shore, the first thing that presents itself to the sightseer after wading through the crowds of squabbling negroes is a large, coarse equestrian statue of the illustrious Gusman Blanco (since thrown down), the only pretension to art which La Guayra can boast, unless it is the immense patches of rouge and powder which bedaub the cheeks of every third of the young women one meets, for certainly the houses and streets were made when architecture was in apprenticeship. The interior of the town is miserably disappointing compared with the magnificent sight which the harbour presents from the sea. The streets are inconveniently steep and narrow, rendering them almost impassable for any vehicle, being more like large drains made to carry off the enormous flow of water which rushes down the mountainside in the rainy season. The appearance of the people of La Guayra is scarcely more prepossessing to the foreigner than the place itself. Those who are not of the dark, woolly-headed negro breed belong to the slim, tall, elegant Spanish dandy type, but differing from their Spanish relations in possessing a much deeper shade of color and a peculiarly sinister expression of features, which, when excited by anger, becomes almost fiendish, giving the visitor an impression that these are scarcely the people to trust himself with in a lonely road on a dark night. A burning sun every day, striking on a dry, sandy soil, runs the thermometer up to over 100 degrees in the shade, and renders the heat almost unbearable: this considered—with the want of all convenience in the house, and the uninviting appearance of the people—putting all sarcasm aside, the most charitable would scarcely be justified in advising La Guayra as a health resort for invalids.

CHAPTER III

WE WERE DELIGHTED TO learn that the latest novelty here is a railway from La Guayra to Caracas, the principal town of Venezuela. We gladly took tickets to the far end, pleased to escape from the heat and at the same time to see the country. If a tunnel could be drilled through the mighty mountain, the distance from the port to Caracas would be five miles; but the railway is twenty-seven miles in length, winding about amongst the mountain passes in the most fantastic zigzag crotchets, gaining in the twenty-seven miles an altitude of over a mile. The train is made up of the engine, one first and two second-class carriages, mere frames, to catch as much as possible of the sultry breeze. The front of the engine is provided with two bags of sand, and a boy on each side put the sand on the rails providing the wheels should revolve without making progress in the steep ascent.

After the usual ceremony which accompanies all kinds of business in this country, the last portly old dame, with an enormous basket of fruit and some chickens, was effectually stowed away in a corner and we started on the journey; at first along the shingly beach, passing a horde of miserable tumbledown huts, then through a fine plantation of coconut palms for several miles of level road. Here began the ascent of the mountain, and at the point where we lost sight of the fine sea view, together with the harbour and town of La Guayra, we had already gained a quarter of a mile in height. Still we continued—here winding around enormous boulders, further along crossing deep ravines of five hundred feet in depth on flimsy bridges over which it seemed scarcely advisable to trust human life, at one point creeping along the mountain side with a height of half a mile above and as much of almost perpendicular precipices below, amongst scenery that would vie with the Alps in grandeur, but where the breaking of an axle-tree would probably submit us to a fate compared with which the Tay Bridge accident would be merciful.

The passenger cannot fail to notice the extraordinary structure of the tunnels: at some points where a more than ordinary splinter of rock comes in the way, a pigeon-hole had been drilled through the hard stone and left without any superfluous padding of brickwork, and so the scenery and the structure of the railway continue all the way to Caracas—so admirable, in fact, that no visitor who comes to La Guayra should miss the sight. On arriving at Caracas we were prepared to feast our eyes on the usual incongruous collection of tumbledown mud huts so peculiar to these parts of South America, and the reader can imagine our agreeable surprise when we steamed proudly into a smart little station of quite European pretensions, with clean cemented platforms ornamented with flowers and creeping plants, and thronged by an aristocratic class of people who appeared by their dress, at least, to be fresh arrivals from Paris. On leaving the station a pretty church of elegant design, built on a slight elevation, attracts the attention of the sightseer by its spotless white towers. Five minutes' ride in a tramcar brings us to the large commodious houses and wide streets of the principal part of the town. The largest square, Ox Plaza, although somewhat small and cramped in comparison with the size of the buildings surrounding it, is gay with flowers, and two large splashing fountains in the gardens of the municipal buildings do their best to give the place an air of coolness in spite of a sun sometimes more than oppressive. The Presidential residence and Government offices are buildings of excellent design and substantial construction. One side of the plaza is taken up by a large college for high-class scientific education—an institution which is a real ornament to the situation. It is a pity that Venezuela does not possess more such.

Fine large *magasins* and stores, several excellent hotels, restaurants *a la francaise*, and so much convenience for business and pleasure are to be found in the pleasant little Venezuelan capital, that if there should be a European who still entertains the idea that there is no society to be found in South America but wild Indians, he will do well to pass a week at Caracas to improve his education. For my own part, the thought that the *Phantom* was perhaps already under weigh made it impossible for me to get more than a glimpse of the town, hastily swallow a cup of the celebrated Caracas coffee, and take a return ticket for La Guayra. I would have willingly stayed to collect the lovely Cattleya Mossier, which is found in plenty growing on the branches of trees in nearly all the mountains around Caracas, and is now to be had with the greatest ease, for the Indians bring large quantities of plants into the city for sale at a very nominal price, instead of the poor plant-collector having to brave all the dangers of the forest (as in other districts) only to obtain a few dozen of plants. One thing struck me as being more extraordinary than all the peculiarities of the people, country, or constitution—that is, that on a railway where every mile presents a thousand dangers no enterprising life assurance company had so far speculated on human vitality as to issue assurance tickets.

In the descent of this single line of goat's-track the magnificent scenery appears even more beautiful than on the upward journey, and the track itself, if possible, more dangerous; for the passengers cannot help wondering where we would stop, providing the brakes failed to act, on a railway which descends a mile in twenty-seven miles of distance. On arriving at La Guayra, we quickly engaged boats for the ship and got on board just as the *Phantom* was firing a parting salute, no doubt to do honour to the officious custom-house officers. We were quickly on our way for the harbour of Puerto Cabello, meanwhile congratulating ourselves that we had received the value of our seventeen shillings with compound interest.

A few hours' sail, always in sight of the rugged coast of Venezuela, brought us to the harbour of Puerto Cabello, a large old-fashioned lighthouse in the form of a Chinese pagoda, and a still older castellated fort whose hundred pigeon-holes bristle with pigmy cannon, which seem more fit subjects for a curio museum, or to be used in some mimic theatrical representation, than to be of any service in modern warfare. These are the first and almost only objects of interest the situation affords for the traveller. The harbour being commodious enough to admit of ships coming to land, we dispense with the services of the black boatman and walk on shore. Mr. Conn, the excellent British Consul, is always ready to welcome visitors, but the very ordinary and somewhat neglected appearance of the town does not offer much temptation to voluntarily stay long in Puerto Cabello. The harbour affords excellent convenience for the exportation of coffee, minerals, and other products of a large tract of country, and a large amount of business is done. Everyone here seems to be as much on the alert to turn a penny as the people of Caracas are to display a new suit or a bonnet. Two small public parks, both crowded with gorgeous flowering plants, give one an idea of the almost spontaneous vegetation of these parts. In one of the gardens are twelve magnificent palms, each towering to a height of nearly one hundred feet, specimens of exquisite beauty, enough to make the least covetous wish that they could be transported just as they are to Hyde Park or Kew Gardens. The only pity is that the last time the people of Venezuela indulged in a revolution, a quantity of the bullets intended for other purposes pierced the stems of the palms and disfigured them with many ugly marks. For those who care to see the country, a well-made line of railway runs from the port to the town of Valencia; or, better still, take a horse and ride to the nearest village on the hills, a journey of about three hours, where the beautiful scenery and rich vegetation of the wild, uncultivated forest amply repay the exertion. As the *Phantom* was lying in port for the night, within a short distance of the fort, those who passed the time on board were treated to a peculiar concert, at first novel enough, but eventually disagreeably monotonous, in the fort, now used as a prison. There are something like three hundred unfortunates who, for the time being, are deprived of the privilege to roam the wild hills of Venezuela. They are guarded by a dozen sentinels, at equal distance from each other around the fort. It seems to be the duty of each one of these to cry out, at the top of his voice, the two Spanish words, "Centinela, alerta!" every half-hour of the night from sunset to daylight, leaving an interval of two or three minutes between each one, beginning with the first man and continuing until the circuit of the fort is made. Perhaps the most amusing part of the system is the difference in the tone of the various voices. The first one will roar out the password in deep, sonorous tones. No sooner has this died away on the still night air than the next one begins with a shrill piping treble; this, in turn, giving place to another who, in a soft singing voice, prolongs the two words to twice their ordinary length; while a fourth, seemingly impatient at being disturbed, jerks out the words in a sharp military rattle, and so on until the twelfth one pronounces them all "alerta" in a tone at least an octave higher than his predecessors. As the vessels are moored almost directly under the walls of the prison, this half-hourly repetition of so extraordinary a comedy renders sleep utterly impossible, and we were not sorry when next morning the *Phantom* steamed out to sea and so gave us a chance of a nap in the cradle of the deep.

Our next calling-place was the island of Curacoa, and in the short sail from Puerto Cabello nothing occurred worth the attention of the reader. To the traveller whose business is to investigate the beauties of foreign lands, the first impressions of the island are anything but satisfactory. As far as the telescope can reach nothing is to be seen but an expanse of sandy desert or barren rocks, and these, if not entirely devoid of vegetation, only produce a weedy scrub. However, this monotony is soon relieved by our coming in sight of the whitewashed walls of the old-fashioned Dutch town. Two well-garrisoned forts form a sufficient protection to the town and harbour.

On passing the Dutch ensign which floats from the top of the fort, the captain of the *Phantom*, in pursuance of certain laws of maritime etiquette, politely dipped the Union Jack three times in the water, a compliment which was as politely returned by the Dutchmen answering the salutation in the same form. The harbour, although presenting a most gay and busy appearance, is somewhat small and cramped, and it was with considerable exertion that our little *Phantom* was brought near enough to the quay to do business. The principal parts of the town are built on each side of the narrow harbour; besides this, a kind of canal branches off into the other parts of the town, cutting the streets at right angles. The harbour as well as the canal is crowded with small boats for the convenience of passengers who are obliged to be crossing and recrossing from one street to another. These boats, generally a kind of punt, are a most primitive cockleshell contrivance, which, however, at one time may have been a Dutch patent. They are perfectly flat-bottomed, and not more than a foot and a half deep, reminding one very forcibly by their general appearance of a large drinking trough. The mode of propelling them is scarcely less comical than the craft itself. The oarsman takes up his position standing in the stem of the boat, with a piece of wood in the form of an overgrown mustard-spoon, which he wriggles from side to side in the water in imitation of the action of a fish's tail. For the price of a few tiny coins, something less than half a farthing each, crowds of people of all classes in search of business or pleasure are conveyed from street to street, if not with the greatest swiftness, certainly with the greatest security, as, up to the present, an accident has never been known. The language spoken here is perhaps the most curious of the novelties which attract the attention of the stranger on arriving at Curacoa. The extraordinary arrangement of sounds called Creole-Dutch strikes upon the ear as something between the howling of dogs and the cackling of poultry, an arrangement of gutturals and nasals equally as difficult to describe as it is to understand; it appears to me to possess neither rules nor system, but, should it have both to the initiated, it is certainly devoid of beauty of euphony. The people seem to be preoccupied with a quiet industry so peculiar to the character of the Dutchman. Scores of women are employed in making a kind of straw hat of soft white grass, very inferior, however, to those made in many parts of Colombia. Another class of industry carried on here on a considerable scale is the manufacture of gold and silver ornaments in filigree work, and, considering the great want of convenience and machinery, many of the specimens are very beautifully made. Although there is very little of importance to make anyone regret leaving the little dream town, we were abruptly called away by the shrill whistle from the *Phantom* before we had time to get a fair look around.

CHAPTER IV

AFTER SOME LITTLE DIFFICULTY, we were again out to sea and making for the port of Savanilla. On our way thither we were aroused before sunrise with the news that we were passing in sight of the Sierra Nevada of Santa Marta, and there was a possibility of seeing the sun rise on its perpetual snow. We had not long to wait. A considerable time before the first rays of sunlight appeared across the water—it was still the dull twilight of early morning with us—those who were looking towards the mountains could distinguish the summit gradually become brighter as the first sunray fell upon it, until the mighty mass of ice and snow shone like a coronet of monster diamonds, and this appeared more striking and beautiful because of the huge base of the mountain being still almost in darkness.

However, as the *Phantom* was going full speed, we were not long in being out of sight of the Sierra Nevada, each one sorry that so beautiful a scene should be so transient. Keeping along the rugged coast, we were soon in sight of what is called the harbor of Savanilla. If this had been the entrance to the greatest penal settlement in the world it could not have been a more barren and desolate-looking place. As far as the eye could reach nothing was to be seen but bare rocks and sand, and there was not a vestige of a town or even a hut in sight to show that the place was inhabited. The *Phantom* dropped anchor, I supposed, on speculation, nothing being likely to welcome us but a host of screaming pelicans fishing from the rocks or the crowds of ugly vultures in their strange funereal garb continually wheeling over our heads in search of some corpse. The shallowness and muddy appearance of the water showed that we were really anchored in the delta of the River Magdalena. Here I intended to disembark, in order to profit by the means of communication which this river affords with the interior of this part of Colombia, but on looking around I must say my ardour was somewhat damped. To all appearance this could be no other than the abode of savages. However, considering the old adage that "faint heart never won fair lady," I went below and quickly packed up my traps.

Upon reappearing on deck I was informed that a small tender was coming off to the ship from a station hid behind a bluff, and in three long hours after the issue of the proclamation the little machine appeared alongside, having occupied all that time in making a distance of about four miles. It is absolutely beyond my power accurately to give a description of this rickety and antiquated piece of marine architecture, called the *Funza*; I only wish it could be exhibited in London for the edification of our modern boat-builders and engineers. In the year 1810, the hero, Bolivar, fought for the release of his countrymen from the Spanish yoke. I am persuaded that at that time this craft may have been one of his gunboats, but, if so, he must even then have bought it secondhand.

It would scarcely be doing justice to the progress of the country not to mention here that, in the four years which have elapsed since my first landing, the *Funza* has been laid aside and its place taken by a smart little boat of more attractive appearance and more substantial workmanship. However, after bidding good-bye to the most excellent and kindly captain and officers of the *Phantom*, I went on board the *Funza* with a few more passengers, all Spanish-speaking people, whom we had taken on board in the West Indies. Each one stowed himself away as best he could, on the top of his baggage, in what I call the stoke-hole of the engine, prepared to wait the three mortal hours which would elapse between leaving the Phantom and arriving at the station. I will endeavor to describe the whole of the journey from here to the town of Barranquilla, so that whoever may be disposed to follow me in this part of the coast of South America may not run away with the delusion that he is going to disembark at Cannes or Brighton. On arriving at the station, we drew up to the side of what appeared to be the companion ship of the *Funza*; across this we passed with our baggage into a shed, consisting of a roof and four posts, where all the luggage is weighed. After this the boxes are seized by a crowd of copper-colored Indians and carried off, if you like to pay them, to where the train is standing. Here all those useful adjuncts which a European finds so necessary and convenient in a station, such as booking-office, refreshment-rooms, stationmaster's and porters' offices, are deemed superfluous, and the train is moored on the bare open ground. This station is called Salgar. More recently a new port has been made, called Puerto

Colombia, and, although still only a very temporary landing-stage, it can boast of many more conveniences than Salgar.

The whole town of Salgar is composed of six or seven of the worst mud huts I have ever seen. These huts cannot be described as being either round, square, or oval, but are made of sticks plastered with mud and thatched with palm-leaves. A few copper-coloured, naked children, a few dirty, half-naked women, and a score of horrid lean pigs, more resembling hyenas, make up the tout ensemble. One more item which I have overlooked—that is the house in which is sold the spirituous liquor of the country, called *anisado*. In this house are congregated porters, engine-drivers, and passengers, all intent for the moment upon the one object of quenching the terrible thirst caused by a tropical sun striking on the dry sand. When the last man had swallowed his dram, we were told in sharp, squeaking Spanish to take our seats, and soon the ponderous machine was put in motion. The whole of the distance from here to Barranquilla occupies about an hour, and the entire railway is laid through thick jungle, novel enough to the foreigner, but, compared with the magnificent forests to be found in the interior, only mere scrub. Finally, we arrived at Barranquilla; and now comes the question of passing our baggage through the Customs. In every port in the world I suppose this is a source of much trouble and annoyance to passengers, but above all at Barranquilla; and for anyone to arrive in possession of two guns is almost sure to result in the confiscation of one of them. I arrived here on a Saturday, and found it impossible to pass my baggage through the Customs until Monday; so, leaving my few traps under the lock and key of the officers, I went off into the town to what is called the Hotel Francais, by no means the Grand Hotel of the place, but a respectable lodging-house, kept by a kindly French matron. The food supplied in the hotels of Barranquilla is somewhat extraordinary to the taste of a foreigner—of which I shall have more to say later—but the bedrooms I can scarcely pass over here without a remark. These are as large and commodious as it is possible to make them, taking up the entire space from the floor to the top of the house; not being encumbered with any furniture, so as to leave them as airy as possible, and render the heat somewhat tolerable. The bedsteads are about the only things which detract from the fearfully bare and comfortless appearance of the place, and these bedsteads might be mistaken by a careless observer for monster meat-safes, being such a curious combination of gauze and laths, the practical use of which only becomes apparent at night as a protection against the myriads of hungry mosquitoes which swarm the place.

Early next morning, being Sunday, I went for a stroll to get a look at the town. I found it large, apparently of about some thirty thousand inhabitants, admirably situated on the bank of a natural canal at the outlet of the Magdalena, and so calculated to receive the whole of the product of the enormous tract of country drained by this magnificent stream. But, apart from its excellent position for export and import trade of every kind, there is very little to recommend Barranquilla as a residence for Europeans. The heat is oppressive, and the streets are filled with a kind of white sand which, on the least breath of wind, rises into the air in blinding clouds. The houses in the suburbs of the town are somewhat tumbledown and unsightly, mostly thatched, but the profusion of beautiful plants which almost hide many of them makes up for the want of architectural beauty. Many of the principal streets, as well as the plaza, have been very much improved lately by the construction of more elegant houses, and the popular South American bullfighting arena has been removed from the plaza to a more out-of-the-way position. Notwithstanding the very commonplace appearance of the houses outside, many of them inside are fitted with the greatest richness and good taste, possessing an easy luxury so peculiar to people of Spanish descent, and admirably adapted to the climate. As a rule, apart from bedrooms, boudoirs, and kitchen, each house possesses a special saloon which serves for reception, ball, and drawing-room, gay with gilded lamps and mirrors, and rich with luxurious carpets and lounges, besides rare paintings and bric-a-brac that would grace the drawing-room of a Rothschild. Enterprising traders have stocked the town with immense shops and stores; but instead of the visitor being entertained with the pleasing pastime of looking into shop windows, he is met at every turn by dismal-looking iron gratings which serve in their place, the immense variety of merchandise being only visible on entering the store.

Barranquilla seems to be progressing socially and commercially as much as any other town in the Republic. Amongst the oldest of the foreign pioneers, everyone visiting the coast is familiar with the names of Mr. Joy and Mr. Stacey, Englishmen who are respected and beloved alike by foreigner and Colombian, while Mr. Cisnero, a rich Cuban, seems untiring in forming schemes for improving the commerce and adding to the convenience of the town. A tramway has lately been constructed through the principal streets. This is not only very useful, but is well patronised; and while I write, machinery for the electric light is in course of construction. The telephone is already fitted in the offices of all the principal merchants, and the great advantages which Barranquilla possesses of communication with Europe will, I have no doubt, soon place it on a level with more advanced cities. Rumours are constantly heard of the unhealthy state of the town: they are generally founded upon the idea that because the climate is hot it must be unhealthy. In the various years I have known Barranquilla I have never seen a case of infectious disease originate here. Most of these cases are brought from alone the coast or from other parts of the valley of the Magdalena. The well-to-do families here are not only cultured and educated, but very often display much personal attractions. Some of the ladies are represented in the adjoining photograph dressed for their annual festival, called the Carnival. The common people are of a light copper colour, seemingly half negro and half Indian, but with very little to recommend them either in form or intelligence.

One of the greatest difficulties a foreigner finds on arriving here is the system of small bank-notes and other kinds of money in circulation. Native gold coins have almost disappeared, and since the last revolution few, if any, have been coined in Colombia, most of the large business transactions with foreign countries being made by bills of exchange. If an Englishman or North American arrives with a few sovereigns or twenty-dollar pieces, his best plan, taking into consideration the rate of premium above the price of native money, is to go to the Bank of Barranquilla, or to the office of Mr. August Struntz, the estimable agent of the Royal Mail, and there buy the paper money of the country according to the rate of exchange. This fluctuates very much with the demand for gold coin. I have sold English sovereigns at the rate of 125 per cent, premium; or for 100 dollars of English gold I have received 225 dollar-notes. The notes in circulation above one dollar are five, twenty, fifty, and one hundred dollars in value; while the dollar note may be divided into ten parts, each small note being called one real, worth about twopence-halfpenny in English money. The next higher in value is called two reals, worth at the rate of exchange current about fivepence. The dollar is further divided into a five-real or half-dollar note, worth one shilling. These, with several nickel coins of small value, make the whole system very intricate and very confusing.

I was detained in Barranquilla several days, much against my will; but at last, learning that a boat was preparing to make the journey up the Magdalena, and this being the best way of getting to the interior of Colombia, at the same time affording an excellent sight of the scenery on the river, I hastily packed up my little luggage, which, by the way, was not very cumbersome, consisting only of a saddle and necessary horse harness, a change of linen, and a gun. A Hyde Park rambler, or a tourist to the English lakes, might think so scant a wardrobe scarcely sufficient to make him presentable for a six months' journey; but allow me to suggest to anyone tempted, by business or curiosity, to make a similar journey, to bear in mind that dress-suits and tall hats are as much out of place in a South American forest as a pig in a drawing room, and a wait-a-bit thorn is no respecter of persons or material.

CHAPTER V

THE BOAT WAS ADVERTISED to leave at half-past seven a.m., and approaching that time the way to the wharf was all astir with clumsy vehicles ploughing their way, almost up to their axles in sand, bearing passengers and baggage. I remarked that whatever luggage the passenger possessed besides, everyone seemed to be provided with a large roll of muslin, a large bottle, and a piece of peculiar-colored matting. The muslin was for mosquito-curtains; the bottle contained at least half a gallon of rum to kill the microbes and counteract the bad effects arising from the water of the Magdalena, besides satisfying a secret propensity which many Colombians possess for *Tragos*—a Spanish word which might be easily interpreted as "a drop o' the cratur." The piece of matting was destined to supply the place of a bed. While dusky porters were noisily stowing away bales and portmanteaus, and sharp native gentry were disputing with them about the price, I had time to look over the boat. There are on the river altogether some thirty of these craft, for the most part large and commodious, built, as I would call it, in two stories, being flat-bottomed, and drawing only about two feet of water. The floor of the lower story is level with the water; about half the front part of the boat at this level is taken up by an enormous stack of wood, used for fuel for the engines. In the middle is the space for cargo, while further on is the driving gear for the large stern paddlewheel. Above this, on the next floor, is the accommodation for passengers, a few cabins on each side and a large saloon in the middle, whilst the prow is reserved as a space for recreation. On the roof of this again are built the cabins of the captain and officers. The three sections carry the construction up to a great height, considering the little depth below the water. The whole being built as light and airy as possible, and gaudily painted red and white, has somewhat the appearance of a travelling menagerie to Europeans, although very pretty and admirably adapted to the situation.

About midday everybody on board seemed to have got all they required, so we started down the narrow arm of the Magdalena which leads from Barranquilla into the main river. Here we passed the majority of the other riverboats, lying either waiting to be dispatched or to be repaired. Here, too, we came in sight of what appeared to me to be the public baths and washhouses of the town. For a distance of about a quarter of a mile along the side of the canal large trunks of trees are placed at intervals of a few yards from one another, and at a depth of three or four feet in the water. Here at least a hundred or a hundred and fifty half-naked women and children, laughing and talking, splashing and screaming, were engaged in washing the linen for the more wealthy people of the town.

This is done by alternately dipping the clothes in the water and then pounding them lustily on the trees in a way that would make an English housewife tremble for the safety of her coarsest towels, not to speak of the possible welfare of muslins and cambrics. Leaving the washerwomen, we followed the canal down towards the sea in order to reach the main river, and, once in the main waters of the Magdalena, the scenery was very beautiful. Looking seaward, a wide expanse of white water rolls swiftly along to mix itself with the blue of the ocean, while ahead of us the flat roofs and tall, red, pagoda-like towers of the town of Barranquilla, standing out in relief against a background of a thousand leagues of trackless forest, furnish a sight at once fantastic and picturesque. On looking around amongst my fellow-passengers, I found as cosmopolitan a company as could be imagined—several Germans, a Russian, a Frenchman, and a family of Peruvians. The usual band of Italian peddlers it is customary to meet with in every part of the world was here in full force, but the majority, in point of numbers, were what may be styled well-to-do Colombians. These vary in appearance from the coarse, thick-set type of the Indian to the slim, elegant gentleman of Spanish descent, with pointed mustachios and high heeled boots. Each one was busily occupied in arranging of his or her effects to the best advantage considering the small space allotted for each person. Soon, however, the soft, musical treble of the French and Italian languages, mingling with the deeper bass and tenor of the German and Spanish, gave one to understand that each was bent upon making the best of the situation, irrespective of difference in creed or language, name or station. Although we were placed on a platform immediately above the boiler and in close proximity to numerous antiquated, misplaced steam-pipes, the absence of any uncomfortable motion of the boat, compared with the disagreeable churning of a sea-voyage, and the tempering of the heat by a soft breeze smelling of a thousand flowers from the forest, make the first impression the traveller receives of navigation on the Magdalena anything but disagreeable.

Whilst I was thus engaged in making something like an inventory of the people, the situation, and the surroundings, the bell sounded for dinner. Perhaps it may not be out of place here, for the sake of any who may care to make the same journey, to mention how the inner man is cared for on these river-boats. The viands, although somewhat extraordinary to the taste of a European, are as good as the country affords, and well suited to the situation. In the first place, to prove that the soup is no spurious imitation, each plate is furnished with two or more turtles' eggs, which float on the top as a kind of trademark. These on first tasting them are scarcely as good as they look; but once the palate becomes accustomed, they prove excellent eating. The fish is probably a small kind of perch which abounds in the Magdalena, but is served so mashed up that it is impossible to say whether it is salmon or lobster. Flesh-meat of every kind is here very inferior, as the heat renders it impossible to keep it for two days without a large quantity of salt, besides hanging it in the sun. All this, together with a very ordinary mode of cooking, renders most of it anything but palatable. The vegetables consist of sweet and ordinary potatoes, together with the cassava root; a variety of tropical fruits and coffee conclude the repast.

The sleeping arrangements on board these boats are of the most novel. On the approach of evening the deck is cleared, and about a dozen trestle bedsteads, covered with a kind of sacking are brought out. One of these is allotted to each passenger, who immediately commences with his arrangements of cords and muslin, so as to hang his mosquito-net in a position to cover the whole of the primitive bedstead and keep the hungry hordes at a safe distance.

If in the journey up the Magdalena the luxuriant vegetation should become monotonous by continuation, this is relieved by occasional villages of true Indian construction. The huts are low, beehive-like structures, with walls of mud and thatched with palm-leaves. Others, probably on the improved system, are made by driving stout bamboo stakes into the ground, about four inches from each other, to form the walls, or, more correctly speaking, the enclosure. This, like the former, is thickly thatched with palm leaves. Inside all ostentatious extravagance in matters of furniture is religiously avoided. Bedroom, dining room, and drawing-room suites here are all supplied, in a primitive manner, by about half-a-dozen blocks of wood, serving the purposes of lounge, chairs, and fauteuil, while a hammock or a few cowhides take the place of bedsteads and eider-down. A collection of gourds and calabashes, with a few cracked bits of native pottery, furnish an inexpensive, and at the same time effective, table service.

However, whatever art has neglected in interior convenience and decoration Nature has supplied with lavish prodigality in the surroundings. For, although each Indian may not exactly, according to the proverb, sit under his own vine and fig-tree, he can yet, even better, build his hut and stretch himself at will under the shade of some magnificent banyan, luxuriant mango, or graceful coconut palm. Although there may be an amusing want of uniformity in the way of one extremity of the house being round and the other square, and an unexplainable want of perpendicular in the walls, the roads between the houses are straight and broad, and in many cases the whole plan of the village is well arranged. The fine growth of trees on each side form avenues as spacious and beautiful in their way as any boulevard in the gay French capital. On the other hand, some are absurdly humble-jumble, and the red-skinned architect seems to have been determined, when choosing a site, to put his neighbor to the utmost inconvenience or satisfy his most eccentric caprices. Most of the people in the smaller villages are of a dusky-red color, with shiny black hair. They are well made and symmetrical, many having regular features, and none with very disagreeable countenances. Some are even pretty. They seem to me to be simple, inoffensive people, caring little about industry and less for fashion. Most of the men are satisfied with a flimsy shirt and trousers, and some are content with less scanty garments; while children of all ages dispense with clothing for the time being.

As we stopped at most of these stations to take on wood, we were inevitably besieged by a crowd of natives, offering us a few fruits, native pottery, monkeys, parrots, turtles, and tortoises for sale. All were laughing and joking, apparently in the highest spirits and the best humour, and, to those who could understand their jargon Spanish, probably criticising severely European novelties in the way of passengers on the boat. Their greatest fault appears to me to be their indolence, and, although possessing considerable civilisation, from constant intercourse with Europeans, I have no doubt their habits are much the same as they were when Christopher Columbus first shook hands with them. Some of the fishing villages present quite a lively scene, and possess quite a fleet of canoes, which are very peculiar in appearance, each one being hollowed out of a single tree, of from twenty to twenty five feet in length, two and a-half feet in depth, and from three to five feet in breadth. It is no unusual thing to see whole families floating dreamily down the river in one of these unpretentious craft, taking with them a load of fish, poultry, and fruit for sale at the mouth of the river; and as they probably occupy from a fortnight to three weeks, according to the state of the river, they must of course take on board both toilet and culinary requisites. Though each boat is provided with short, spoon-like oars, they are only used in crossing the river. The ascent is made by means of long, stout sticks about twenty feet in length. The boatman places his stick firmly on the root of a tree or in the sand of a bank, and then walks sharply back to the stern of the boat half-a-dozen paces, and is followed in turn by his neighbour. Sometimes as many as six men are required, on account of the strong currents, and they continue this arduous labour for a week together, creeping slowly up the side of the river, day after day, under a burning sun.

The traveler on the Magdalena River will not fail to notice many curiosities of the animal as well as the vegetable world. Hordes of enormous alligators swarm its banks on either side; half-a-dozen or more bask on every sandbank, varying in size from five to twenty feet long, and in color from light grey to a sooty black. I have counted as many as thirty on one sandbank, yawning sleepily in the sun, as tame as a herd of cattle, and affording excellent sport to the passengers. But a ball, sometimes two or three, must be well planted to stop one of these lazy gentlemen from shuffling away to die in the bottom of the river out of sight of prying eyes. Large and small lizards dart in and out of the creepers which festoon the riverbanks, but scarcely give one time enough for a shot. Sometimes several hundred of large black ducks, with a kind of sawbill, stand like a line of soldiers, absolutely fringing the sandbanks. They are an easy prey to the sportsman, but when cooked prove tough and unsavory. Long lines of herons patiently carry on fishing operations, whilst flights of small white cranes wheel about in the air, disturbed by the passing boat, or else poise themselves on one foot on a fallen tree, looking like some strait-laced belle in their pure white plumage and delicate elegance. Kingfishers and humming-birds flit from branch to branch, giving us a sight of the primary colors to make up for the absence of rainbows.

The Magdalena is navigable in the whole length—about nine hundred miles—and at a considerable distance from the sea is still a magnificent stream, with a depth which has already swallowed up some of the large steamboats until not even a vestige of the funnels are left in sight. However, in the months of January, February, and March the continued dry season reduces the quantity of water considerably and lays bare miles of sandbanks, sometimes rendering navigation very difficult and dangerous, except to those pilots who, by their great practice, can tell where the deepest channel is with no other aid than their careful observations, which requires no small skill, seeing that in a single flood a running body of water, thirty feet deep, will shift from one side of the river-bed to the other, leaving not more than two feet of water where there was formerly thirty.

When the Magdalena is full of water the steamboats from Barranquilla invariably run the first three nights when making the ascent. After that navigation becomes extremely dangerous, on account of the many large trunks of trees half-hidden in the water.

Late in the evening we arrived at a large village called Remolino, which contains about 2,000 inhabitants, mostly of a dusky copper color and evidently of negro origin. The houses are of a miserable class, all made of mud or wild cane; I did not see a single stone construction. The climate here is bad, being charged with miasma, especially after the rainy season. The heat is also very oppressive.

On account of the river being full of water, and favored with a beautiful moonlight, the boat kept on up the stream. The mosquitoes arriving in hordes, we were obliged to take refuge under our mosquito nets until morning, when we woke up to find ourselves fifty miles further up the river, but, unpleasantly, to find as well that we were wet to the skin with the heavy dew which had fallen during the night. The ordinary route from the river Magdalena to the interior town of Bucaramanga is by means of canoe on the river Lebrija, but, in my desire to get a sight of the South American forests, I left for the time being these more frequented ways and determined to take the path directly through the forest; and with that intention, after three days' journey, I left the steamboat at a small village called Puerto Wilches, situated in one of the most luxuriant and beautiful parts of the valley of the Magdalena. The entire settlement consisted of about two dozen miserable huts. The people by their swarthy color appeared to be half Spaniard and half Indian. They live in a situation where the land is so rich that with the least exertion it would produce two or three crops yearly. In their mud huts the very barest necessaries of life are very scarce for many weeks together. Bread is not to be had, and flesh-meat is equally scarce, excepting game shot in the forest. The principal articles of consumption are maize, turtles' eggs, fish, and bananas.

Here I was treated to a dish which, up to the present, had been entirely unknown to me. This is the flesh of a large lizard, about three feet and a half in length, shot by one of the natives in an adjoining tree. After some trouble in skinning and preparing it, I was induced by the cravings of a well-whetted appetite to put aside all scruples of delicacy or custom and discuss the merits of the flesh of the celebrated iguana, which to many of the natives is a dish of the greatest delicacy. I found the flesh very tender and palatable, and, had it not been for the trouble recently experienced in skinning the scaly gentleman, I might have believed it to be the fattest of some well-reared brood of chickens. I spent three days here preparing for the journey and getting acquainted with the situation. Perhaps what surprises the traveler here is to find in this forest-wilderness several railway wagons and about a thousand steel rails, all in a pitiful state of wreck and dilapidation, caused by the heavy rains. These, I am told, are the remains of a scheme originated by the excellent Colombian general, Solan Wilches, to carry the railway from this part of the river Magdalena to the town of Bucaramanga, a distance of some one hundred and fifty miles. A pity that through political disturbance so admirable a scheme was frustrated. The heat in this part is almost unbearable, and in the rainy season the ground becomes literally a swamp, on account of the constant downpour of rain, which is very violent, often causing yellow fever and other epidemics. The vegetation here is of the richest, and every evening the stately cocoanut and clustering ivory-nut palms are besieged with crowds of brilliant-coloured macaws; swarms of large and small parrots fill the air with their screams; large flights of pink and white cranes wheel about above the river in search of stray fish; while the toucans, with their enormous beaks, quarrel with each other for some favourite fruit, giving the whole situation an appearance at once novel and interesting to a foreigner. On making inquiry about the path through the forest, I was informed that no saddlehorses had passed that way for several years, and that the road was entirely filled up with fallen trees and creepers; besides, there were some eighteen branch rivers to cross—at this time very much swollen with the recent rains. These rivers—of course without bridges—must be crossed by swimming or on the branches of trees. My first preparation for the journey was to engage the services of two natives—real forest rangers as they afterwards proved. These were called by the outlandish names of Don Isidoro Hermenaldo and Don Anastasio Montpulano, but, to somewhat simplify these extravagant and troublesome titles, I christened them, for the time being, the one Bob and the other Tom. Bob, the elder of the two, appeared to be about twenty-three years of age, tall and lithe. His coppery skin and hair of the deepest raven showed that since his Indian forefathers held undisputed sway as Lords of the Forest he had not lost caste. His black eyes possessed a fathomless cunning, no doubt intensified by his profession of the chase, a characteristic which gave a foreigner some misgivings as to his safety in such wily society. His companion, Tom, was still a lad, seeming to be not more than fifteen years of age, of much lighter colour, and, if possible, of a constitution more slim and elegant. In his rolling frolicsome eyes it was easy to read that mirthfulness of character which is peculiar to the free sons of the forest, unfettered by the bonds of education.

Each of my companions was eager to inform me that he was well acquainted with every turn of the path, having been many times that way before, and also was apt in the mysteries of tracking deer and wild pigs, turkey and grouse, as well as the jaguar and tiger-cat, with which the woods abound. Knowing that we were not likely to meet with many inhabitants for more than two days' march, we accordingly laid in a stock of what provisions we could buy, consisting of a few roots of the cassava plant (Jatropha *Manihot*), some flesh-meat and bananas, coffee and raw sugar, together with candles, matches, and a stock of ammunition. Our cooking utensils were an old lard tin and some calabashes, these being very much preferable to the native pottery, which, although very durable, is very heavy. At daybreak on the fourth day from landing we prepared to say good-bye to the people of Puerto Wilches, who, whatever they may lack in culture and resources, certainly are not wanting in hospitality—above all, the excellent magistrate, Senor Don Eugeno Castillo, in whom every stranger will find a willing friend.

CHAPTER VI

AT FIRST THE PATH LAY along the three miles of railway which had been constructed and abandoned several years before. This had now become entirely filled up with creepers and tall grass. Leaving the last rail behind, we quickly plunged into the thick forest, where the road became a mere trail, which made it extremely difficult to proceed. First we were scrambling over some fallen trunks, then cutting our way through a thicket of prickly acacias; sometimes wading up to the knees in ditches caused by the heavy rains; at other times swinging ourselves, monkey-like, from one branch of a tree to another, in order to cross the turbulent, swift-running rivers without wetting our ammunition and provisions. But, even with these difficulties, the path all the while lay through the midst of vegetation of indescribable luxuriance and beauty, Nature's original productions as yet unmarred by the woodman's axe or the ploughshare. Gigantic timber trees, from seventy to one hundred feet in height, festooned to the very summit with creeping Allamandas, all aglow with their golden trumpet-like flowers, mixed and varied with the scarlet stars of the *Tacsonia Van Volxemii*, or the rich blue of the Ipomaea and the undergrowth of palms of the elegant Phoenix and Cocos families. These were supplemented by a carpet of the most beautiful mosses and low, flowering shrubs, while on the banks of the streams the deep crimson flowers of the creeping *Cyrtodeira fulgida* contrasted beautifully with its richly penciled leaves of velvet and gold—everything that could illustrate the glories of the vegetable kingdom, with the exception of Orchids; and for these I scanned the trees eagerly, but always fruitlessly, on account of the altitude at which the best Orchids are found being very much above the level of the Magdalena Valley.

But Nature had been scarcely less prodigal in her provision of animal life. Large and small lizards, of the most exquisite markings—some which seemed to possess a coat of mail made of silver and turquoise—disturbed in their afternoon nap, hurried quickly out of sight in the long grass; while birds of every fantastic shape and colour flitted in and out of the feathery palms. Occasionally we came in contact with a colony of large brown monkeys, those missing links of Darwinian celebrity. At the sight of us they set up such a chatter as would almost lead one to suppose that they were discussing on the spot what possible motive could have induced us to venture so far from civilization. The woods were full of a kind of wild turkey, but we were not successful in shooting any. However, we bagged some birds about the size of a hen, which appeared to be a kind of grouse. The sun, already low in the heavens, warned us that it was time to prepare our camp, and in this my two guides proved how well they were accustomed to this kind of life. The forest to these primitive architects supplies everything. While the elder one was cutting some stout poles, the younger one disappeared and as quickly reappeared with an armful of fine creepers, with which the poles were lashed together, first placing my Macintosh on the top, and then a thick covering of large palm leaves, so that in less than an hour they had finished the construction of a commodious shed. Not having been occupied in building operations, I had meanwhile made a fire and prepared the grouse for cooking. These, well boiled with some of the cassava roots, made us an excellent supper, being doubly acceptable, for the long march since the mid-day meal had given us almost wolfish appetites. After supper we prepared each one a small calabash of steaming coffee, boiled in the lard-tin and sweetened with raw sugar. After this each one was content to light his roll of tobacco, and so pass the night by the campfire.

Before daybreak next morning we were astir, and raking together the smoldering embers of last night's fire, prepared our black coffee and roasted some bananas. This temperate repast quickly and unceremoniously dispatched, each one shouldered his load and again we plunged into the dense forest.

We had not gone far before a stream of considerable dimensions stopped our way, for the time offering great obstructions, not so much for ourselves, who could easily cross by swimming, but how to pass our packs with any sort of security offered no small difficulty. Finally, finding a large tree fallen halfway across the stream, by dint of one helping another we were able to pass, and so continued our journey. At noon, as on the previous day, we stopped to cook our midday meal and to rest a short time, for although, on account of the thick forest, the sun did not strike upon us much, still the heat in the middle of the day was extremely oppressive. Besides, the fatigue occasioned by cutting our way through the thick clumps of prickly acacias made us glad to seek a little repose.

Continuing our way, after some refreshment, the track, as on the previous day, lay through the same extravagance of vegetable and animal life. A thousand delicate creepers hung in graceful festoons, and woven into a tapestry compared with which a Gobelin picture would make a poor contrast. After a tiresome march, at the end of the second day we arrived at the only hut which is to be found in all the journey through this part of the forest—and, considering that the nearest neighbors are on every side at least thirty miles distant, the inhabitants of this forest prison, as might be supposed, had partaken considerably of the nature of their surroundings—a hut of the most primitive construction, stocked with a few calabashes, sloth and tiger-cat skins, and blocks of wood. The proprietor of the hut, an old hunter, showed himself extremely friendly, and immediately offered us part of the provision nearest to hand, being some cassava roots, bananas, and bread made of Indian corn ground between two stones. Here we passed the night, the whole of next day, and the following night as guests of the kindly native, being obliged to make this delay on account of a terrific thunderstorm and heavy rain, which continued to fall all day.

As the forest dried up somewhat in the night, early next morning we prepared ourselves again for the journey; but as the provisions which we had brought with us were all exhausted and we could buy nothing more here, we left somewhat depending on the chance of meeting some stray wild pig or anything else which might come within range of our guns. From the hut which we left in the morning to the next hut in the forest was a distance of twenty-four miles, and there it was not certain that we should meet with any inhabitants. We continued along the track with much the same surroundings as formerly up to midday, and as we had seen nothing to shoot but some monkeys, we were reduced to the necessity of making our lunch off some pineapples and other fruits, which are plentiful enough. About one o'clock in the afternoon, while still following the track, we left the thick forest and suddenly broke into what appeared to be a large dried-up lake, the ground being perfectly flat, and a kind of fine, powdery sand covering the entire surface.

The only vegetation consisted of patches of miserable scrub here and there. Having no exact information of the breadth of the plain, it appeared to me that we had walked about five miles when we again struck into the forest. These five miles we had passed with the greatest difficulty: an almost vertical sun heated the sand to a great degree and rendered the atmosphere stifling; besides, at each step the foot sank into the powdery mass up to the ankle. Nothing living was to be seen, but at short intervals we passed the tracks of wild cattle, as well as many footprints of the jaguar and tiger-cat, which are plentiful enough in all this part. The footprints of cattle surprised me, as large wild animals such as the buffalo or bison are entirely unknown in these forests. However, my companions informed me the race had originally escaped from some settlement on the edge of the forest. After some rest we again struck on the path, being anxious to reach the hut before night. Darkness came on suddenly about half-past six o'clock, as is usual in this latitude, and, unfortunately for us, with night the thunder began to roll through the sky, while the black clouds, illuminated with bright streaks of lightening, warned us that a storm was approaching. We still kept on our way, in hopes of reaching the hut, but in vain; quickly drops began to fall, and then the fearful torrent which followed would make one believe that a cataract had broken loose over our heads. The scanty shreds of clothing which each one wore were soon soaked, my top-boots as quickly filled and the water ran over the tops, while the track became a stream. Everything which we carried became running with water. The light pith with which the natives so easily produce fire, together with the matches I had, were equally rendered useless. We were exhausted with the fatigue of the day's march, and were without fire or provisions, and the violence of the storm rendered it almost impossible to construct even a temporary shelter. Besides, without this, to stop short of the hut was to hazard our lives. The two natives behaved admirably, going first, scrambling through the tangled brushwood, the track being only discernible at intervals when the brilliant lightning lit up the gloomy surroundings.

About two hours after the storm broke upon us, impelled by sheer desperation, we arrived at the hut—a tumble-down shed, as may be supposed, with the rain coming through in every part of the roof; but, to our joy, there was a lire in the place, and, on examining further, we discovered three natives huddled up in the driest part of the shed. These were travelers like ourselves, on their way from Bucaramanga to the

River Magdalena. They had arrived before the storm, having had time to collect wood and cook their supper: of the little provisions which they possessed they sold us some cassava roots and a little raw sugar. Quickly disencumbering ourselves of our dripping remnants of clothing, we boiled some of the raw sugar in water—this makes an excellent and refreshing drink when it is drunk warm. Being somewhat refreshed with this, we next prepared the cassava roots and supped well on these, and my companions heaping a large pile of wood on the fire, we waited for daylight, making ourselves as comfortable as possible under the circumstances, not unmindful to Providence that we were better there than in the open forest without shelter.

Morning revealed to us the woods in all their grandeur again, with scarce a trace of the hurricane which had swept over us on the previous evening. Our first consideration was to dry everything we possessed by spreading it in the sun; meanwhile our companions, who were going in the opposite direction, had breakfasted and taken to the track. The preparation of our baggage delayed us until nearly noon, but the guides said that we should find another hut at about twelve miles' distance. Towards evening we came in sight of the Andes, having nearly crossed one-half of the magnificent valley of the Magdalena: Before sunset we had reached the hut, which was situated about half a mile up the side of the mountain on a slight level, a situation which commands one of the grandest sights it is possible to see. On the right the magnificent forest-plain stretches out towards the sea for two hundred miles, and on the other hand as much. The river Magdalena is navigable for large steamboats about nine hundred miles, and from this point of the Andes on a clear day there is at least five hundred miles of the valley visible, while directly in front may be seen the mighty range of mountains of Antioquia and Bolivar at a distance of a hundred miles more. The river may be seen from this point like a gilded serpent gliding away down towards the sea, its silvery coils contrasted beautifully with the sombre green of the forest.

This evening we were more fortunate than the night before. Here we met with a party of Colombians engaged in taking out gutta-percha, and they offered us every hospitality which their scanty resources afforded. We started away next morning more refreshed and in better spirits than on the previous day. This hut is called Las Mercedes, and is situated about half-way up the mountain, from which the town of

Bucaramanga lies some twenty-five miles on the other side. Before mid-day we reached the top of the mountain. From this elevation the view is even more beautiful than before, and the clear, bracing air gives us an idea that the range of hills is at least four thousand feet high. From here as well we began to discern the cultivated land and small villages on the outside of the forest. After about four hours more of a most toilsome march down the side of the mountain, where the track is scarcely discernible on account of the thicket of creepers, we emerged into cleared ground and a fairly beaten track. Passing several straggling huts, we finally reached a large house covered with red tiles, an excellent specimen of the better class of country-house in the interior of this part of Colombia, the owner being a coffee-planter of considerable importance. We arrived here in the evening, and near to the house we were met by a crowd of young men and women, each one bearing a large basket filled with coffee-berries, each workman being paid according to the weight of fruit picked during the day. The berries are afterwards spread out on cemented floors in the sun, where the outside rind of the fruit is taken off and the coffee-beans cleaned by first beating them in a mortar and then subjecting them to a kind of winnowing process.

The excellent Colombian proprietor of the estate (which is called El Naranjo, or the Orange Tree) treated us with every kindness, which was doubly welcome after the rough life we had just experienced. I passed the night here, and early next morning engaged mules to proceed on my journey to the town of Bucaramanga. The road from this point to the town is supposed to be good, which, in fact, it is, compared with some of the roads. But, for anyone who has not an idea of what is called a road in the Republic of Colombia, I may describe it as a mere track, worn into existence by the continual passing of mules, with packs and riders, often taking a roundabout way where a near one is at hand, or climbing over a stony precipice when, with the least forethought, it might have been avoided; besides, in the rainy season, the clayey soil becomes impregnated with water, and works into a kind of substance in which the mules sink up to the saddle-girth, which makes it impossible for any other beasts but such as are accustomed to these roads to extricate themselves.

On leaving El Naranjo the road lay through numerous plantations of coffee, cocoa, and sugarcane, broken at intervals by large patches of scrub. The farmhouses are supplied with numerous buildings for drying tobacco, crushing sugarcane, and preparing what is called *panela*. This is the juice of the cane boiled, poured into molds, and left to cool. These molds are square, and the pieces of sugar are invariably small cakes about the size of a box of sardines. As the juice has undergone no process of refinement, the sugar produced in this way is generally very dirty, and of a color as dark as roasted coffee-beans. This is produced in very large quantities, and is entirely consumed in the country, either for cooking or in making the native beer, or *guarapo*. After about nine miles' riding, we came to a small village called Canta Abra. This soon showed us how much the difference of elevation had to do with the social condition of the people, compared with the natives of the valley of the Magdalena. Instead of the strong Indian or negro type, so marked in the natives of the low land, the Colombians here are fair-skinned, good-looking, and well dressed. Although the village is one of the smallest in the vicinity of Bucaramanga, it boasts of a good, large Roman Catholic church and several well-built houses, but of course all of mud, or what is called *adobe*. Here we breakfasted in true Colombian style—a piece of salt beef and cakes made of Indian corn; besides, we had the inevitable cassava root and coffee. The coffee, made here on a coffee estate, as may be supposed, is an exquisite beverage, possessing all the rich aroma which the berry loses by a long sea voyage. After breakfast we started away at a rattling pace, which did not slacken until we had gained the summit of a hill from which were easily discernible the strange half-Moorish, half-Spanish towers of Bucaramanga.

CHAPTER VII

THE RIVER LEBRIJA IS THE finest river draining the state of Santander, a tributary of the Magdalena, rising in what is called La Mesa de Juan Rodrigues, in the Eastern Andes, at a height of about nine thousand feet above the level of the sea, passing the town of Pie de Cuesta on the north-east side, and running through the old Spanish town of Jiron, following the department of Soto in the state of Santander, and emptying itself into the Magdalena at a place called Bodega Central, a small boat-station of comparatively recent construction. Perhaps there is no better means of getting a good experience of what canoe life really is than by taking a journey on this river. Going up, there are the long, weary days with a burning sun and cramped privation, dragging the canoe over the rocky shallows; and in descending, there are the fearful rapids and whirlpools, where many of the canoes, with their freight and passengers, are lost every year. Thousands of bags of coffee are annually brought down from the interior on this river, and a corresponding number of bales of manufactured goods are carried up. The town of Bucaramanga contains about fifty thousand inhabitants, and every one of these who would make a journey to the coast, however distinguished or delicate—from the polished Spanish lady to the hardiest Indian—must submit to a six days' imprisonment in one of these miserable craft on the river Lebrija, or another branch river called the Sogamoso, where the circumstances are pretty much the same, the only way to this large interior town being by way of these rivers, with the alternative of the overland route, which is a hundred miles' tramp through the forest, with men bearing provisions. When I made the ascent of the Lebrija I left the Magdalena steamboat at Bodega Central, which is largely owned by two estimable merchants, Messrs. Lopez and Navarro, and is remarkable for the immense thatched warehouses, crowded with piles of bags of coffee, hides, gutta-percha, cocoa, plants, and various other products of the magnificent State of Santander, one of the richest, most important, and most progressive States in the Republic of Colombia.

Messrs. Lopez and Navarro, besides owning most of the canoes on the river, also have several small steam-launches, which ply on the

Lebrija to a place called Estacion Santander. I took passage as far as the steamboat went, and we left Bodega Central at four a.m. in the little launch called *La Primera*. We steamed across the Magdalena and entered the mouth of the Lebrija, daylight coming about half-past five, and with it a sight of more natural beauty than I had seen before. I greatly enjoyed the wild magnificence of the forest and the enormous timber-trees festooned with such a profusion of gorgeous, flowering creepers, supplemented by thickets of graceful palms and bamboos. The banks of the river are intersected at intervals by small streams, which drain the adjoining forest and sluggishly empty themselves into the main river. At each of these outlets a sight presents itself which would enchant the most stoical naturalist. Several huge alligators lounge lazily in the soft mud. As far as the eye can reach up the creek, crowds of ducks are actually huddled together, each one brushing his neighbour to get fishing-room. The principal species is called by the Colombians El Pato Real, or Royal Duck—a wild muscovy, weighing sometimes from eight to ten pounds; colour, a greenish black, with white patches on the wings. Another, which is called in Spanish *Pato de Aguja*, is one of the divers, having the body black and the long neck covered with a peculiar ashy-coloured down; the long, snake-like neck tapering to the fineness of a penknife at the end of the beak. I shot some of both species, and they proved excellent food.

The low bushes trailing in the water of the stream are literally white with small cranes, wistfully waiting for some careless fish, while the tall trees are bristling with large cranes of various classes. The osprey, or fishing eagle, and kingfishers complete the collection. I would gladly have secured a photograph of so interesting a sight, but as the little steamboat arrived opposite to them they invariably rose like a cloud, and, after wheeling around in the air several times, alighted a few yards off to wait until the disturbance was passed. The streams above-mentioned run into the Lebrija at intervals, and, as we passed each one, all on board seemed carried away with a desire to possess some specimen of these myriads of beautiful waterfowl. Many large trunks of trees torn from the banks and brought down the river by floods made the navigation very difficult, as we experienced when, about mid-day, our little boat ran afoul of an enormous log, and it was only after two hours' work with axes and bars that we were at liberty to proceed.

Besides this, there is the delay occasioned by taking on wood for the engines.

However, eventually we arrived at Estacion Santander—something like sixty miles in about ten hours. The appearance of the village is not very prepossessing, the houses being of the most miserable construction, made of stems of the wild cane bound together with creepers, like huge birdcages, thatched with palm leaves. These huts are almost entirely occupied by native boatmen, or, as they are called in Spanish, *bogas*. Occasionally, these sheds are made extra long, and divided into compartments by a latticework of wild cane, each division containing at least one family. The situation is even worse than the village, being the edge of an extensive swamp covered with rank grass, in many parts intersected with pools of stagnant water, and in the rainy season being entirely flooded. Here the night dews are very heavy, and the air is continually charged with miasma, making it almost impossible for any European to live long in such a climate, the heat being also unbearable and the mosquitoes legion. This is the principal station for canoes on the river, and they are tied up to the bank in great numbers, from the most primitive hollow tree that will hold two men with difficulty, to the clumsy construction which carries fifty bags of coffee and six men. Something like two hundred native boatmen live in the huts of this station. They are of the coarsest negro type, and about as low a form of civilization as it is possible to find, excepting a tribe of wild Indians. They are absolutely averse to any kind of work except that of the canoe, so that whatever social advancement might be offered to them they would not accept it. However, in the management of the canoe they are invaluable, for out of the hundreds of times they make the journey of the river, shooting the terrific rapids at lightning speed, besides hauling the canoe and cargo over fallen trees, with which the river is almost impassable, or in the dry season working in the water cutting channels, not two per cent, of the canoes and freight are actually lost.

For two days after I arrived at Estacion Santander I was not able to get a canoe going up the river, so, to pass the time in so miserable a situation, I went alligator hunting. Two or three species of alligator abound in all the swamps and rivers, but the most common is the large cayman, which grows to a length of from eighteen to twenty feet, and attains an enormous bulk. We had not far to go before we met with several, and this being the breeding season, they were especially hasty-tempered when compared with their usually sluggish disposition. The female scratches a hole in the sand, a few yards away from the water's edge; here she deposits a large number of eggs—from twenty-five to seventy. I have never found them more than one-foot-and-a-half deep, but always on a sandbank considerably elevated above the river, to prevent them being washed away with the floods. The months of February and March is the time when the alligators deposit their eggs, and it is extremely dangerous to go near the female when so doing, the huge animal, disturbed on the nest, first gives warning of hostile intentions by uttering a loud, hissing sound, like a snake, and by puffing out the neck and opening her monstrous jaws. The intruder who, after these warnings, disregards them, must be a good shot and armed with a good weapon, or otherwise very careless of his life. Although the natives are careful not to expose themselves too much in the water of the river, many people are annually killed by alligators. If a fisherman advances too far into the water, or some unfortunate Indian upsets his canoe, he very often falls an easy prey to the lurking monsters which lie at the bottom of the river in perfect shoals, watching for large fish or whatever living being may stray within reach, and once between those terrible teeth all hope must be abandoned, for I have never heard of a single escape. The armour on the back of the alligator is made of a quantity of stout bone plates under the skin; these are very difficult to penetrate; but the vulnerable parts are the eye and behind the shoulder—a ball well planted in either situation is certain to kill. Our day's sport ended with two males and one female, all of which the natives managed to drag to the station and skin, only utilizing the skin of the underside of the animal. One of them measured seventeen feet and the other fifteen feet—fairly good specimens, but not very large. Next day I set about getting together the natives for the canoe, and providing a stock of dried fish, salt beef, cassava root, bananas, and some coffee, together with cooking utensils, fishing-nets, guns, and ammunition. It was also necessary to construct an awning over the canoe, to somewhat break the glare of an overpowering sun.

The following day, after much delay, I mustered my company of six men, and we started up the swift-running, muddy stream, not forgetting to take with us a large bottle of native spirit, called *aguardiente*—a liquor made from the sugarcane, of a disgusting taste and unbounded strength, which one would say, in ordinary phraseology, is warranted to kill at a thousand yards. Indeed, the native boatmen are so accustomed to the use of this drug that the alcohol eventually loses its effect upon them. An amusing instance happened on the journey up the river. I had taken a bottle of alcohol with me to use in a spirit-lamp, with the object of boiling water to make tea on the journey, but by some mistake a pint bottle of alcohol was given to the native boatmen instead of the *aguardiente*.

Unfortunately for me, they drank every drop of the fiery substance, with no worse effect than to slightly intoxicate them. I only discovered the mistake when I went to seek the alcohol to make my tea and found instead only a bottle of native spirit which would not burn. The boatmen seemed to leave their huts with the utmost reluctance, and proceeded very slowly. In their homes they wear some clothing, and many of them even a decent suit; but once away from the village, they discard every vestige of clothing, in order to be more ready to jump into the water when pleasure or necessity prompts them. We had not gone far up the river when the natives, struck with a fit of laziness, took to the woods, and left me with one man in the canoe to do the best I could. Of course, it was impossible for me to proceed without them, so I took my gun and went off into the forest to see if there was anything to shoot. There are plenty of wild pigs and the tapir, called by the natives *La Danta*, but it is difficult to get a shot at it without having some dogs. I was not long in coming up with some of the natives engaged in fishing in a small lake, about two and a half miles from the river; the water muddy and stagnant, but so full of fish that there was no need of the wily patience generally employed in angling. The only difficulty was to get the fish off the hooks quickly enough, so eager were they to bite. In about two hours we had taken as many as four men could carry. The fish were of three kinds, one about twelve inches long, covered with silvery scales, having a very small mouth. This is called by the natives Boca chica, or little mouth; it is the fish that most abounds in all parts of Colombia, and is excellent eating, probably a kind of perch. The next is La Dorado, or the gilded fish, from eighteen to twenty inches in length and five inches in girth; the flesh of this is inferior to that of the Boca chica, but the appearance is most wonderful; the scales, especially around the head, are of a glistening yellow, making one believe it is wearing a suit of gold-gilt armour. The other, a short, ugly fish, with formidable rows of teeth like a miniature shark, is called by the natives Moncholo; this fish proved the best food. By the time we had gathered our booty together, the sun, low in the heavens, warned us that it would soon be dark, and we hurried back to the canoe as quickly as possible. The natives gathering wood and making a fire, we all partook of boiled fish, bananas, and a little coffee. After this, everyone stretched himself on the sandbank and prepared to wait until morning, amid crowds of hungry mosquitoes. Although the natives dispense with everything, having only the sky for a roof, yet to a European the heavy dews are very injurious, and it is always a good precaution to erect a kind of awning of palm-leaves to prevent the clothes being soaked during the night.

By daybreak everyone was astir, and the bananas and black coffee were enjoyed with as much gusto as an Englishman would enjoy the proverbial ham and eggs. We were soon moving slowly up the river, the natives working, as usual, without a particle of clothing in a vertical sun, only now and then stopping to jump into the river to refresh themselves with a bath. On account of the swiftness of the river, it is impossible to use oars except for crossing; but the labour of pushing the boat along by the sandbank is more tiring, so much so that no European would be able to endure it for more than a few days. In the forenoon I had excellent shooting from amongst a flock of parrots and waterfowl. The banks of the river were alive with the beautiful egret-cranes, and the trees full of macaws, some scarlet and blue, some blue and yellow. About mid-day we partook of our usual rations of fish and bananas, with palm-wine. The process of making the palm-wine is somewhat curious. The largest of the trees are selected and cut down; then, when the tree is laid flat, the whole of the leaves which fall uppermost are cut away until the white young growth in the middle of the tree is laid bare. Out of this part a large, square piece is cut, sufficient to leave a hollow which will hold at least a quart of water; then the hollow is carefully covered over and the palm-wine maker waits until next morning. As a rule, when he returns he finds the cavity filled with a whitish liquor, having the appearance and taste of lemonade, only a little sour, but very refreshing and beneficial.

About three o'clock we arrived at a small station of two or three huts. Here the natives learned that there was a herd of wild swine in the vicinity, so all progress up the river was stopped, as the boatmen would go no farther that day. Everybody was on the alert for a hunt; so all the dogs of the place were got together, and two rusty old guns, which were all the station could muster, most of the natives being armed with lances, and what is called here the machete, or cutlass. Away we started into the forest, trampling down and cutting through the beautiful stre-litzias, delicate palms, and gorgeous creepers. With the help of the dogs, we were not long in finding the track of the herd, and then we went on about an hour before we came up with them. The natives wore next to no clothing, but mine was reduced to shreds in the desperate struggle with the thorns and creepers. The first sign of the herd was given to us by a pattering sound and a very rank smell, besides the barking of dogs. Presently we appeared to have dropped into the middle of them, as every part of the forest seemed alive with wild pigs. There must have been at least three hundred, rushing backwards and forwards in the wildest confusion, some of the natives darting through amongst the trees with the dogs, trying to keep the herd together, others firing as quickly as they could reload their guns, and some using their cutlasses to kill as many as possible. After about a quarter of an hour of the most exciting fight that it is possible to imagine, the whole of the herd that remained unwounded had disappeared, leaving us to despatch the wounded and gather up the dead. When we were able to collect them together we found seven as the proceeds of the raid. These were shoul-dered and carried in triumph to the camp. The cooking process was not a long one. The flesh of the young peccary is excellent, but that of the older ones is somewhat inferior; the largest weigh from thirty to forty pounds, and are very much like small, domesticated pigs, of a dull black colour and having coarse bristles; the head and nose are very long in proportion to the body, and the feet very small. Herds of peccaries abound in these forests, in such large quantities that the natives can always have fresh meat when they are not too lazy to hunt.

It being already dark when we returned to the camp, I contented myself here for the night, and we started by daylight next morning, without any breakfast, as the natives would not wait; so, as a passenger has absolutely no authority over them, I thought it best to let them go when they were in the humour. We took with us a good supply of the flesh of the peccaries, and later, when the boatmen felt inclined, we stopped at a sandbank, and while one party lighted a fire and prepared breakfast, the others went in search of turtles' eggs. The nests of the turtles are discovered in a very curious manner. To an ordinary observer nothing is to be seen but an expanse of flat sand, but the men returned with over two hundred eggs, the means of discovering them being to pierce the sand at intervals with a stout stick to find the cavity containing the eggs. The turtle comes out of the river during the night and scratches a deep hole in the sand; in these holes the eggs are deposited all in one night, and not, as is generally supposed, in several nights. I have read accounts of more than a hundred eggs being laid by one turtle; but I am not inclined to believe the story, as the oldest native told me he had never found more than three dozen in a nest of one turtle. It often happens, however, that two or three deposit their eggs so close together that they are easily mistaken for one nest.

About mid-day we arrived at a small village called Papayal, a canoe station of little importance. Here I bought some provisions, and stayed about an hour. When I was ready to start again I found it almost impossible to persuade the natives to proceed with the canoe. After very much trouble I got them on board, and we continued lazily up the river. That night we camped on a sandbank; the opposite side of the river being the edge of a thick forest. The boatmen lighted a fire and partook of supper, and then, probably fatigued with the toil of the day and the unbearable heat, they were soon stretched on the sand sleeping heavily. I was unable to sleep on account of the mosquitoes, so I sat down to contemplate the grandeur of the situation. The full moon lighted up the dense forest with a kind of weird, unnatural beauty, and a stillness reigned around that would make one believe we had camped on the territory of the dead. Towards midnight what appeared before so deserted became suddenly animated; large flights of white cranes arrived, and poised themselves on the branches nearest the river, while as many more of the tall grey ones took up quarters on the edge of the sandbank, wading as far as their long legs would allow. The alligators, which, up to the present, had kept carefully under the water, began to make an appearance, first poking their heads cautiously out, and then dragging their long bodies out on the sand, while a crowd of about a dozen turtles raced out of the water. The opposite bank was not less animated than the one on which our canoe was moored. I could hear the peccaries grunting and rushing about in search of food. Several deer and one tapir came down to the water to drink, being distinctly visible in the clear moonlight. The occasional sharp bark of the ocelot and the deep growl of the jaguar, together with the mimic roar of the howler monkey, and the low, prolonged wailing of the sloth, seemed fit accompaniment for so wild a place. I lay down to rest, leaving them in the height of activity, and when daylight came nothing was to be seen of my midnight visitors but footprints. All this day we kept on steadily up the swift-running stream, little of importance taking place, and in the evening we camped again on a sandbank. From here we could see the long, blue line of the tops of the Andes away on the horizon, but still at a considerable distance, on account of the winding of the river.

CHAPTER VIII

NEXT DAY WE CAME to some rapids, which extended a considerable distance, where the water rushed down a declivity with terrific velocity. Here the natives were obliged to bring the canoe to the bank on the shallowest side, and, all jumping into the water, literally lifted the boat up through the foaming torrent, wading up to the neck in the water and making a great noise, shouting to each other in their bad Spanish by way of encouragement. When we had got clear of the rapids we stopped to rest, and while we were there three canoes, laden with coffee, came down the river and joined us. I was curious to see how they would shoot the rapids—a mile of rushing, foaming torrent, intersected at intervals by enormous trunks of trees, which, at some time or other, had been brought down the stream, and were now firmly embedded in the banks. These obstacles caused the angry weight of water to eddy and boil like a monster caldron. The principal danger to the canoes shooting these rapids is the probability of being dashed to pieces against some of these hidden destroyers. The boatmen seemed to understand fully their desperate danger, and as the first canoe moved away from the bank I could hear them encouraging each other. The first canoe was loaded with forty bags of coffee, and no sooner was the frail bark pushed off from the side than it was caught in the current. The descent from where we were to the still waters below occupied about five minutes, and so great was the velocity that had the canoe only jarred with any of the projections of the banks it must inevitably have been dashed to pieces. But the skill of the natives is so great that they guided the whole of the canoes safely into the calmer waters below, and, once clear of their danger, gave an exulting shout which we could hear above the roar of the rapids. After little more progress, night came upon us again. I had been fortunate through the day in shooting some ducks, so we had no lack of food.

Next day we started by daybreak, and as we neared the higher part of the river we found it in many places very shallow, and on this account we had a piece of sport which was quite new to me. This was a race with a large fish, called by the natives *savalo*, somewhat like a salmon. They seem to be fond of feeding in the shallows on the edge of the sandbanks, and at a considerable distance away we could see their movements in the water; so directly we brought the canoe opposite to them, the boatmen jumped into the river and gave chase, driving them as much as possible into the shallowest part. The chase was most exciting, six natives to four fish, dodging each other with such surprising agility that they only lost one, the others being killed by a stroke of the machete, which the natives use with such dexterity. It was impossible for me to learn the scientific name of this beautiful fish. It is very symmetrical in form, about two feet and a half in length, and is covered with scales of a peculiar shape and enormous size, each one larger than a crown, and glittering like burnished silver. I have seen the same fish grow to a size of seven feet long and two feet six inches in girth. When cooked it proved somewhat unsavory, and considerably less palatable than beautiful.

About mid-day on the sixth day from starting we arrived at the foot of the Andes, and about four o'clock in the afternoon, after great cheering and salutation from one lot of boatmen to another, we landed at the port called Botijas—no very inviting place, but at least a relief to get liberty from the cramping confinement of the canoe. A large sheet-iron warehouse and a few miserable thatched huts are all that the inhabitants can boast of to make up their village. This place is proved the most unhealthy. One or two Colombians are placed here by the merchants of the interior to look after the despatch of cargo by the canoes. These poor fellows are only able to stay about a month, and then seek the higher ground to recruit themselves from the terrible malarial fever which inevitably fastens itself upon them. All the produce going down the river in canoes arrives here on mules, and some hundreds may be seen at a time loading and unloading bags of coffee, bales of gutta percha, or cases of plants. Very few stay more than one day, on account of the climate. As the village is situated at the foot of the mountain, the ascent can be made in about two hours to a large country-house called El Volador, built on a ridge of the mountain several thousand feet above the River Lebrija. On the top of the mountain the air is fresh and cool, and the climate good. From here to the town of Bucaramanga the journey can be made in two days, over a tolerably good mule track, which passes through the midst of many beautiful plantations of coffee, tobacco, and sugarcane.

What appears most extraordinary to the traveler when he mounts up to the top of the range of mountains which overlooks the town of Bucaramanga is to find a large town of about fifty thousand inhabitants at so great a distance from any port and so thoroughly isolated in the tops of the Andes. The natural situation is very beautiful, the town being built upon an extensive plain, about 3,000 feet above the level of the sea, and this plain entirely surrounded by high mountains, and these mountains for a considerable distance up the side adorned with pretty country houses, each one with a patch of sugar-cane, a plantation of coffee or tobacco; while as far as the eye can reach is an extent of pastures enriched with splendid herds of cattle and troops of half-wild horses, while the tops of the mountains tower into the clouds, which shroud them day and night with a veil of impenetrable mist. The plain on which the town is built, as well as most of the adjoining land, has long been celebrated for the gold found there, and especially in the old-fashioned village of Jiron, where the Spanish conquerors found sufficient to load their ships with hoards of treasure. The gold is very good; but many of the mines discovered by the Spaniards have been lost or abandoned, and those which remain, although they still yield largely, are not so profitable as in former years.

Once inside the town of Bucaramanga the whole arrangement is most novel. The streets are very narrow and paved, being highest at the sides, and having a stream of water running down the middle of each of the principal thoroughfares, serving at once for the supply of the town and for sanitary purposes. The water is generally taken from some stream in the nearest mountainside, and brought by conduits to the town, where, in various branches, it is made to pass through all the principal streets, and again, in hundreds of branches, is carried to form the many beautiful baths and fountains which are found in the houses of the, rich Colombians. As a rule, the houses which form the suburbs of the town are miserable tumbledown constructions, and the streets are so even that they will scarcely admit of wheeled vehicles passing along them, so that every kind of conveyance, such as cabs, omnibuses, wagons, etc., is entirely unknown in this mountain retreat.

The houses are principally one story high, and the long streets, in which the whole of the houses seem to have been made from the same model, give the place an appearance of dull sameness perfectly unbearable to a European. But once inside the door of one of the best of these houses everything is changed. The apartments are built to open into a square or garden, generally cooled by a splashing fountain, and planted with innumerable sweet-smelling flowering shrubs and gorgeous orchids. The largest hall or reception-room takes up the whole of the square adjoining the street, so that on the one side the windows overlook the traffic and passers-by, while on the other side large folding-doors open to a wealth of floral beauty. These saloons are often most gorgeously furnished the richest gilding, the choicest pictures, carpets from Persia and draperies from India, with an extravagance in silver and bric-a-brac almost impossible to believe could ever be found on the tops of the Andes. Two sides of the square are taken up by the bed-rooms, which also open into this floral promenade, the remaining side of the square being reserved for the dining-room; and on account of the perpetual mildness of the climate this hall is left entirely open on one side, so that the well-to-do Colombian, instead of requiring floral decorations to adorn his dinner-table, literally dines under the shade of orange-trees laden with blossom and fruit. Huge gardenias, whose crowds of waxen flowers fill the air with their exquisite perfume, with large clumps of the lovely orchid *Cattleya Mendelii*, give to the whole group a masterly finish of colour. The business houses of Bucaramanga are quite equal to any in other parts of Colombia, and a large trade is done in cotton goods and hardware, as well as immense exportation of products of the country. There are many excellent hotels; a club, telegraph and telephone offices, post-office and banks are to be found; while the latest novelty for the tops of the Andes is to be the electric light, the machinery being, at the time I write this, on the way from Europe to be carried up the mountains on the backs of mules.

Apart from all this, what strikes the visitor as the most curious of all the curiosities of Bucaramanga is the market, which is held some three times a week in the principal plaza, an extensive square in front of the church. Here every Saturday may be found such a collection of products of a diversity of character as is rarely met with. Flesh-meat is sold under small tents to protect it from the blaze of the sun, while bales of gutta percha, sacks of coffee, and rolls of tobacco are heaped up in the midst of stores of merchandise from Europe, potatoes and Indian corn, raw sugar and bananas, oranges, peaches, and figs, all jumbled together topsy-turvy. The people are no less remarkable for their diversity of color, character, and nationality. Here a sharp German trader may be seen bartering with a Red Indian over a cent in the price of a pound of coffee, or some elegant Colombian lady jostles with the rough Indians of the hills in the excitement to secure some delicious fruit or extra fine capon. Sisters of Mercy, Roman Catholic priests, a large percentage of Germans, a few Frenchmen and Italians, together with the educated Colombians, negroes, and half-breeds, are all intent upon making the best bargain. The principal trade of the town in the importation of manufactured goods is in the hands of German traders, of which there are many important houses, as well as a few rich Colombians. The educated society of Colombia has always been noted for its capacity and intelligence, and Bucaramanga, besides possessing several good schools and a college, has given to the country from time to time many celebrated men, both in literary, political, and scientific pursuits, while the State of Santander undoubtedly has a population of the most industrious class of people to be found in Colombia.

Doctor Aurelio Mutis, one of the most popular inhabitants of Bucaramanga, as well as of this State, was educated in medical colleges in London, Edinburgh, and Paris. He is a man of most affable character, coupled with the sprightly vivacity of the men of his race, polished and accomplished in the highest degree. He speaks fluently Spanish, English, French, and Italian. As a medical man he is equally in request in the palace of the millionaire and the Indian hut; and it is said that in his long experience in this large town of so diversified a class of inhabitants none ever asked for his help and was turned away. As a political man he has lately become famous, having been for a short time Governor of the State and then Secretary for Education. He is at present in England acting as Consul for Colombia in the port of Southampton.

My journey was made in search of the fairy tribe of Orchids, and as up to the present I had not even seen a single plant of value, I was delighted to learn that the early botanists had found the gorgeous *Cattleya Mendelii* growing around here in profusion. Now, however, through the immense exportation of these plants, not a single one is to be found within many days' journey from here on mules. I accordingly set about hiring mules for myself and baggage, and again started off in search of the capricious flower. This time the way ran along the valley of La Florida, passing on the way large works in progress for taking water to wash the gold-bearing sand of the vicinity. Nearly the whole of the land along the valley is carefully cultivated; the beautiful crops of waving sugarcane, maize, and tobacco, and the rich pastures stocked with peaceful herds of cattle, give one a feeling of European surroundings. On each side of the valley the mighty peaks of the Andes tower up to the clouds, all bristling with forest. Twelve miles of the most agreeable riding brought us to an old Spanish town called Pie de Cuesta, or in English, "Foot of the Hill."

This place contains about 12,000 inhabitants—peaceable, industrious people, mostly employed in making cigars and straw hats, as well as in agricultural pursuits. In the whole of my variations in life and circumstances I have found no town or village I have liked so much as the quiet, beautiful, dreamy old town of Pie de Cuesta—about 3,500 feet above the level of the sea, with something like twelve hours of day and twelve hours of night all the year round, a mild, balmy air which is never oppressively hot or disagreeably cold, an abundance of pure water, and a rich variety of tropical fruits. The majority of the houses are commodious, and even spacious, while the people, at the same time possessing all the sprightly wit of the modern Colombian, are free from that knavish, over-reaching disposition which develops into a system of roguery in most of the outlying mountain villages. The natural situation of the town is as admirable as the climate and the people are agreeable. I was glad to find the beautiful *Epidendrum atropurpureum* covering the walls around the houses and flowering in profusion; and here also I found one of the most beautiful of the South American birds—the scarlet and black tanager. This is called here by the natives the "Cardinal Bird," and, compared with a flock of these, no Roman prelate ever made a more brilliant effect. It is a small bird, about the size of a starling, the wings and tail of a velvety black color, while the rest of the body is a most intense scarlet; the otherwise black beak is adorned with something like plates of ivory on each side of the lower mandible. I was delighted to obtain several good specimens of this gaudy little woodland gem.

The mule track, on leaving Pie de Cuesta, keeps along the fertile banks of a stream, in a southern direction, for some miles, and then commences an ascent of about one thousand feet, until we reach what is called La Mesa de los Santos, an extensive plain where the wild Indian must have ranged and camped at will in the time when the Spanish yoke was unknown. The vegetation consists of a tall, rank herbage, with occasional scrub, intermixed with thousands of the beautiful *Sobralia leucoxantha*, with rose and white flowers of the colour and substance of a *Cattleya Mendelii*, but so difficult to transport that very few of the plants are known in England. The inhabitants of this magnificent plain are mostly cattle-keepers, who are possessed of the best class of horses to be found in this part of the country; they are also celebrated for their splendid horsemanship.

Every morning they may be seen careering over the expanse of prairie with a lasso of about thirty yards long, of raw cowhide, tied to the pommel of the saddle, and wearing a pair of very wide leggings, which are strapped around them at the waist and float in the wind on either side something like a lady's dress. These half-breeches, half-leggings, are called in the Spanish *zamarros*. The saddle is as peculiar a production as the rest of the arrangement, being raised up very high at the front and back, so that the horseman appears to sit in a chair. A square piece of cloth, with a hole cut in the middle for the neck, is thrown over the shoulders; this, and a wide-brimmed straw hat, complete the curious costume of a Colombian cattle-ranger. One side of La Mesa de los Santos is bounded by immense precipices, some of them over two hundred feet in height. These are the haunts of several birds of prey, most notably the condor, or, as it is called in the Spanish, *El Buitre*. This gigantic bird has a spread of wing of six feet, and has strength to rise from the ground with a fair-sized calf. I have seen them wheeling around at a considerable height, and they seem to alight on the ground very rarely. The natives' mode of killing them is to slaughter an old horse or other large animal on the edge of a precipice, and the quick-sighted bird is down upon the carcass before life is quite gone; the natives wait in ambush until the monster bird is gorged with the flesh, so as to be unable to rise quickly into the air. The lurking Indian watches his opportunity, and with the agility of a deer falls upon the condor with spears, and generally comes off victorious. On the ledges of these precipices, where the eagle and the condor make their home, the lovely *Cattleya Mendelii* has grown in profusion since the memory of man. Even when the first plant-hunter arrived, these dizzy heights offered no obstacle to his determination to plunder. Natives were let down by means of ropes, and by the same ropes the plants were hauled up in thousands, and when I visited the place all that I could see of its former beauty and wealth of plants was an occasional straggling bulb hung as if in midair on some point only accessible to the eagles.

I left the place impressed with the magnificence of the scenery, but disappointed in my search for plants. Continuing over the plain, we arrived at a small village of ancient Spanish construction, called Los Santos, situated on the very edge of a declivity of about one thousand feet. In the valley below runs the turbulent little river Subi, formerly called by the Indians the Chicamocha. On the opposite side of the valley mighty precipices rise to the same height as the one on which we stood. It seems as if the river had once flowed over the level plain, but floods, during centuries, had cut out the terrible chasm which opens so suddenly to the traveler. The distance from the one line of precipices to the other, at the top, is about a mile and a half, and the mule track was down the mountainside, across the river, and up the other side, on to the plain beyond. The descent occupied about an hour and a half of the most perilous winding about amongst rocks, and creeping along shelving ledges, where the mules, with one false step, would have been dashed to pieces. At intervals we came to small huts, the occupation of the owners being to keep goats, of which there were many large herds nimbly jumping from rock to rock, cropping the scant herbage which scarcely finds room to grow amongst the crowds of American aloes and other prickly cacti.

On arriving at the little village called Subi, I was surprised at the great change of temperature. Instead of the fresh, bracing air of the plain, the heat here is intense, the thermometer seldom falling below 100° in the shade. The village has lately become a health resort for invalids suffering from diseases of the skin. Many of the patients may be seen all day bathing in the swift-running stream, the waters of which, although coming from the high, cold hills, become warmed in their transit through this burning valley. Here also I found a lovely little bird which I had not seen before—a small creeper about the size of a robin, with dusky-brown wings, but having the breast of a brilliant scarlet, and wearing on the head a crest of long feathers of the same gaudy color, which it raises or lowers at pleasure. I was glad to rest our mules and pass the night here; but long before daylight next morning we began to make the ascent of the precipices on the other side, and by the time the sun was up we had already made half the ascent of the mountain. The view from here is very beautiful; the stupendous rocks may be seen on one side of the chasm, with the immense prairies of La Mesa de Los Santos stretching away as far as the eye can reach, losing themselves in the horizon. To the south, one of the tributaries of the river Subi, after creeping along the plain for some distance, suddenly falls over the rocks with a hound of a hundred feet, resolving itself into spray and rainbows in the chasm below. I had been informed that *Cattleya Mendelii* was still to be found in quantities on the eastern range of the Andes; so, after leaving the precipices of Subi, I turned off in the direction of a small village called Curiti, at the foot of the rang of mountains so celebrated for orchids.

Here I left my mules and proceeded on foot. The vegetation is somewhat semi-tropical, lovely ferns and selaginellas being very luxuriant, as well as the feathery bamboos, but with an absence of the fine, rich timber-trees and towering palms of the lower grounds. Here, amongst the scores of hummingbirds which flit from flower to flower, I made the acquaintance of one which I had not seen before, and which, I believe, was the prettiest I had ever seen. This is known in England as the Blue Sylph, having two long feathers in the tail like those of the swallow, but of the most resplendent metallic blue. Here also the rare and beautiful Swallow-tailed Kite may be seen wheeling gracefully overhead all day, but far out of gunshot. I had not far to go before I was rewarded with the object of my search in the myriads of Bromeliacece and orchids which literally cover the short, stunted trees and the bare points of rocks, where scarcely an inch of soil is to be found.

The most magnificent sight for even the most stoical observer are the immense clumps of *Cattleya Mendelii*, each new bulb bearing four or five of its gorgeous rose-coloured flowers, many of them growing in the full sun or with very little shade, and possessing a glowing colour which is very difficult to get in the stuffy hot-houses where the plants are cultivated. Some of these plants, considering their size and the slowness of growth, must have taken many years to develop, for I have taken plants from the trees with five hundred bulbs, and as many as one hundred spikes of flowers, which to a lover of orchids is a sight worth travelling from Europe to see. Apart from the few extraordinary specimens, the orchids, as a rule, are very much crowded and mixed up with other vegetation. The accompanying picture, from a photograph taken on the spot, represents a tree growing in its natural state in the forest.

The higher branches are covered with a long, white lichen; a little lower is an immense clump of Tillandsias; while the branch on the right hand is inhabited by some Oncidiums. The next plant, lower down, is a nice piece of *Cattleya Mendelii*. The whole of the mountains at the time of my visit were crowded with the famous parasite. Like most of my predecessors, I was tempted to bear away a large quantity of the coveted plants, besides exploring the mountains and enjoying much of their beauty.

CHAPTER IX

MY NEXT JOURNEY WAS in search of the popular orchid *Odonto-glossum crispum*, which, I had been informed, was to be found so far in the interior of Colombia as the department of Cundinamarca, on the slopes of the Andes in the vicinity of the capital city. To reach this place would necessitate a journey of about two hundred miles on horses or mules. This mode of travelling: is more monotonous, more tiresome, and more expensive than the adventurous life of the forest. The general direction of the track is south, but it has many deviations, going through the State of Santander, a short distance in the State of Boyaca, and terminating in the State of Cundinamarca, passing on the way some twelve small towns and villages, one or two Indian, the others of the old Spanish style, many of them being extremely pretty in situation and construction. Several of the villages are celebrated for the desperate conflicts which took place between the Spaniards and the natives of Colombia in the terrible War of Independence.

I will only particularize one or two of the principal towns; to enumerate more would only be to weary the reader with repetitions. After a long, toilsome day's journey over the rocky heights of the Andes, I arrived at the town called Sanjil—a town of some 14,000 inhabitants, beautifully situated on the banks of the River Fonce. It was originally peopled by the Guave Indians, and dates from the year 1620. It is notable for its well-built edifices, mostly of stone of excellent Spanish workmanship. A cave is shown full of human skeletons, probably all that now remains of its early Indian owners. Another day's journey over the same mountain heights brought us to the town called El Socorro. This is nearly four thousand feet above the level of the sea, with a lovely climate, built on the banks of a river; it has four churches and a convent, besides many very excellent buildings, and perhaps the best suspension bridge in Colombia, which is very ancient in appearance. This town is notable as being one of the principal places in which the revolution of the Independence commenced. On the 16th of March 1781, when the taxes and ill treatment of the Spanish Government had become almost intolerable, a peasant woman of the name of Maria Vargas tore down the list of taxes and the Spanish coat-of-arms, which was hung in the plaza, and broke them in pieces. This excited the people so much that, although independence was not proclaimed for twenty-nine years after, this was really the beginning of the war.

Two days of rough riding in the burning sun brought me to a small Indian village called San Benito. The climate of this place is exceedingly good all the year round, being built on a high ridge on the tops of the Andes. I found the people most inhospitable, and the houses mostly thatched with straw and very bad. Keeping along the track, we passed on the way a small town called Puente Nacional, most picturesquely built on the banks of a river, about one half of the houses being on each side. The buildings, as usual, are very good, and a pretty church is an ornament to the place. For five days' journey the track had run through the most miserable class of vegetation. Apart from the curious undulating tops of the mountains, which sometimes extend away into most glorious scenery, nothing is to be seen but a miserable scrub, and the eye becomes weary with the endless expanse of moss and short, stunted shrubs. When we came to some wayside farm or plantation, the clumps of orange trees, laden with their wealth of golden fruit, somewhat broke the monotony. A few flocks of sheep and stray cattle wandered about over the immense waste lands, but an almost entire absence of birds and other animal life gave the tops of the Andes an appearance of desert loneliness. As a rule, in the early morning and in the evening the tops of the mountains are enveloped in thick mist, and the track was scarcely visible. The rising sun gradually dispelled this from the peaks, only leaving straggling patches in the valleys.

At the town called Puente Nacional I was delighted to find a somewhat better class of vegetation commence, and this seems to be the limit of the growth of the *Cattleya Mendelii*, and the commencement of the gorgeous-flowered *Cattleya Warscewiczii*. In the mountains near to this town, in the flowering season of the plants, the display in the woods is most superb. High trees, in some places, are so hung with these glorious epiphytes that very little is to be seen but a blaze of purple and rose. A small Epidendrum with scarlet flowers makes up the finishing touch of colour.

On leaving Puente Nacional, we had not crone far before the track led us to still higher mountains, and here was the division between the States of Santander and Boyaca, near a small village called Saboya.

From the top of this we obtained a magnificent view of the plain on which the city of Bogota is built. This plain is more than one hundred miles in length, and in many places three miles broad; for the most part beautifully level pastureland, or cultivated and bearing waving crops of wheat and barley. Large quantities of potatoes are also grown. We very quickly descended to the plain and arrived at another town called Chiquinquira. This is the yearly resort of thousands of pilgrims, who come to the church to pay their devotions, in the belief that a picture of the Virgin Mary which is here was painted by a miracle. The story runs that a poor woman had coarse cloth nailed in the window of her house to keep out the wind, when one morning she is said to have found the picture miraculously painted on the cloth! The church of the pilgrims, which is called the Church of Our Lady of Chiquinquira, is adorned with great riches in marble, paintings, gold, and precious stones, and it is calculated that the money brought by pilgrims into this place every year amounts to 30,000 dollars, or 6,000 sterling. The climate of this place, which is about eight thousand feet above sea level, as well as the whole of the savanna of Bogota, is cool and agreeable. At this town we are still a distance of seventy-five miles from Bogota, which is three days' journey on horses. After riding all day over a most fertile plain, we stayed for the night at a small village called Ubate, and from here the road is wide and level, and is continually traversed by bullock wagons on their way to and from the capital.

The next day's ride brought us to a large and important town called Cipaquira. The houses and plazas here are of the best and most elegant construction, but of a style which the Spanish emigrant must have learnt from the Moors. The effect of the peculiar tiling and towers when seen from a distant height is most pleasing and fantastic. This town is built on the edge of the immense salt-mines which supply the whole of this part of Colombia with salt, being literally a huge mountain of that substance, which was known to the earliest Indians. The excavations begin in the side of the hill and run level with the ground, the cavity extending over half a mile, the roof in many places being fifty feet in height—a wall of salt occasionally intermixed with veins of pyrites of iron. The sight presented to the visitor who enters these immense vaults is truly magnificent. Occasional drops of water have covered the roof with myriads of stalactites of every imaginable form of beauty, while the sides dazzle with rock and salt crystals which make one believe one has entered some gem palace or diamond caves. These mines are the property of, and worked by, the Government of Colombia; and although the system of working is somewhat primitive, the salt taken from these hills produces something like one million dollars paper money yearly.

The town of Cipaquira is a distance of thirty miles from Bogota. In the dry season the road is very good, and stagecoaches run every two days. The scenery along the road is most picturesque. For ten miles a line of willows have been planted, and these form a perfect avenue, besides making an agreeable shade, and on each side of the immense plain the continued chain of the Andes rises high and breaks into frowning precipices, giving an increased charm to the surroundings of Bogota. After a delightful ride, I arrived at about two o'clock in the afternoon at one of the suburban villages, called Chapinero. A tramway has lately been constructed from here to Bogota, and the strange mixture of traffic along this road is most curious. The dusky Indian with his old-fashioned pack mule, donkey riders and elegant horsemen, tramcars and carriages, all jostle each other along the dusty road. The entrance to the village is especially pretty; and even along the road the rich Colombians have built beautiful villas, with pleasant gardens and surroundings. Some Moorish, some Persian, and even Indian and Japanese architecture is represented, with an extravagance of Italian marble and paintings scarcely credible, all this making an agreeable entrance to this isolated Andean city.

Entering the city of Bogota from the north side, the visitor is disappointed in finding the streets narrow and dirty, and the houses miserably tumbledown; but in a very short time we arrive at the Park San Diego, a small recreation ground, tastefully laid out, and beautifully ornamented with fountains and statues, the principal one being a full-sized bronze figure of the statesman and soldier Simon Bolivar. The dome and pedestal are of Italian workmanship, very tastefully made, and the whole is surmounted by a gilded condor. The town of Bogota, the capital of what is now called the Republic of Colombia, was founded, according to history, on the 6th of August 1528, and in the year 1540 Carlos V of Spain raised it to the rank of City, with many other privileges. It numbers about one hundred and fifty thousand inhabitants, and covers an area of some two million square yards, situated at an altitude of eight thousand feet above the level of the sea, and only four degrees thirty-six minutes north of the Equator. Except for the slight inconvenience of the rarefied air produced by the altitude, Bogota possesses one of the most healthy climates to be found, having a medium temperature of fifteen degrees Centigrade all the year round. The city abounds in edifices of interest, including a magnificent cathedral. The municipal buildings take up one side of the principal square, the residence of the President of the Republic. In the immense building called the Mint was coined, at the time when gold was as plentiful here as in Australia, one hundred millions of dollars in gold and seven millions in silver coin. There is also an excellent library, containing about fifty thousand volumes, a museum crowded with thousands of natural history specimens and curiosities, besides an astronomical observatory, founded as lately as the year 1803, which claims to be one of the highest in the world. The manners of living and the dress of the people are with few exceptions entirely European, and poodle dogs and perambulators are as much a nuisance on the sidewalks and gardens of Bogota as they are in London. As a rule, in the Colombian towns there is a peculiar spirit of easy indolence and want of stir which paralyses business, and the Colombian's, as well as the Indian's motto is always *mañana* or *to-morrow*. In Bogota, however, there is an exception. There seem to be fewer loafers; everyone appears to be occupied and to go about his business, and, especially in the principal streets, there is quite a bustle.

Continuing along towards the centre of the city, we come to another small park, called Park Santander. This is planted with a profuse wealth of tropical trees and foliage plants, and is the principal resort of the Colombian idler, the luxuriant sand-box trees forming an ample shade. The centre of the park or plaza is ornamented with a bronze statue of General Santander, and the whole arrangement shows the greatest care and good taste. On leaving this park we pass over the first of fifteen bridges, which are all built inside the city over two mountain streams, both of which rush noisily through the principal streets. The business houses are about half-Colombian and half-foreign; they are, as a rule, overflowing with merchandise, drapery goods, and hardware. I believe almost anything may be bought here that is to be found anywhere else, although Bogota is seven hundred miles from the sea-port, and nearly one hundred of this journey is made over the Andes on mule-back; yet the ironworkers from Birmingham, the cotton-workers of Manchester, Benson's watches, Taute's wearing apparel, with Morton's hams and Peek Frean's biscuits, all find a sure representative in Bogota, in spite of the difficulties of mud and mosquitoes which are thrown in the way of the traveller. The French, German, and American houses are nowhere behind in the market. The produce of the country is sold here every day in a large enclosure set apart for this purpose, called the Market, and this forms one of the most complete collections of fruit and vegetables which the world can give. Apples, strawberries, plums, and cherries mix with their tropical relations—pines, bananas, figs, and mangoes; while, on the other hand, potatoes and cabbages are as plentiful here as yams, cassava roots, and pumpkins—in fact, anyone who will take a European cook to Bogota may live in Epicurean luxury. The religion of the capital, as well as of the whole civilised part of the country, is Roman Catholic; but all creeds are tolerated, and in Bogota a very nice Protestant church has been constructed, besides a large number of schools, and colleges. There is what is called the National University, founded in 1867; in this institution every branch of higher education is taught, and the school for medicine in Bogota has long been celebrated. These schools admit something like five thousand students every year, and ten thousand more would be necessary to somewhat advance the educational condition of this immense country. Although there is not much liberty of the press, some twenty-five newspapers are printed in Bogota, several of them daily. The principal and central square of the city is called La Plaza de Bolivar; it is very much more spacious than that of its rival at Caracas. The situation is most agreeable, one side being taken up by the large cathedral, and the other three sides by gay shops, hotels, and imposing municipal buildings; while the centre of the Plaza is occupied by a beautiful piece of bronze, in the form of a statue of Bolivar—perhaps the best work of art to be found in all the city. This was made by the celebrated Italian sculptor Tenerani, at the expense of a rich Colombian, Senor Paris, and placed in Bogota in the year 1846, as a mark of the friendship which had existed between the great soldier and the giver of the statue, as well as to commemorate the many glorious victories won by Bolivar in the service of Colombia. It is a marvel how this beautiful piece of bronze could have been safely transported over the Andes, as everything must be carried on the backs of mules or bullocks.

The ladies of Bogota are very rarely seen outside during the middle of the day, and only occasionally in the evening. But on Sunday morning, about the time of the morning mass, a foreigner taking a stroll in front of the cathedral may get some idea of what sort of people really inhabit this mountain hermitage. Hundreds of women of all ages and every position crowd towards the church. There is the short, clumsy native servant, wearing a dress of all the colors of the rainbow; there is the graceful half perfect form and olive skin. Contrary to the general rule, some lovely blonde will be dressed all in white; but the perfection of the Colombian ladies might be mistaken for a piece of animated marble.

The loose, black, church-going robe lends additional charm to the Venus-like form, and the Spanish mantilla, loosely thrown over a wealth of raven hair, makes a suitable frame for one of the most perfect types of beauty—La Colombiana. However much history and experience remind us that one third part of the country is peopled with the wildest of Indians, the foreigner who takes a turn in the Plaza de Bolivar on a Sunday morning would think they had never been to Bogota. Although Colombian soldiers do not make much of a show, they are celebrated for their straight shooting and valor. In Bogota there is a considerable garrison, together with all the paraphernalia and accoutrements of a standing army. These are not needed to combat with exterior powers; but about every three years they indulge in a revolution or an insurrection against the powers that be, and Colombian kills Colombian, until often very few are left, causing an immense loss of life and property with very little advantage to either party. In times of revolution, however, foreigners who do not mix in the party feeling are not molested in the least, except by the want of communications, and I may say here that for the travelling foreigner there is perhaps no country in the world where he is received with such hospitality and so much friendliness. Both the telephone and electric light have been introduced into Bogota, and a line of railway to connect this city with the Magdalena River has been some time in course of construction; but, if ever it is possible, it will be years before the end is achieved, on account of the immense chain of the Andes between Bogota and the Magdalena, which will require an outlay of some millions of dollars, coupled with the greatest engineering skill, to break through.

The number of inhabitants in Bogota fluctuates considerably with the season. Many of the people possess country-houses, or *campos*, and on the approach of the dry season they leave the crowded town and take to the fields, where each one occupies himself raising crops, tending cattle, or in the coffee and banana plantations. One cause of the difference in population according to the season is that a large number of Indians come in from the hills bringing the produce of their hunting or cultivation for sale in Bogota, and in return buy what little they can afford in the shops, and then leave for their mountain homes till the next season. Another cause is the constant string of foreigners arriving continually from almost every country in the world; these stay a week, a fortnight, or a month, as business demands, and they in turn seek other parts, where the commercial traveler can tell yarns about his experiences in Bogota and the road to it.

The country is governed by the Senate and a Chamber of Deputies, and these are directed by the President. The President, Doctor Rafael Nunez, has held this important position three times, his last term of office extending over a period of six years, which will terminate in July next year. Doctor Nunez does not live in Bogota, but he is represented there by a Vice President, who is invested with acting power in all State affairs, while the President enjoys life in his pretty country home near the city of Carthagena.

President Nunez is now about sixty-six years of age; he was in early life President of the State of Bolivar, also Consul for Colombia in Liverpool and Havre, besides filling the important positions of Minister of Finance and Prime Minister of his own country. He is a man of great force of character and refined literary tastes, and speaks fluently several languages.

All the environs of Bogota are pretty and picturesque, especially the two peaks called Monserrate and Guadalupe—in the immediate vicinity and overlooking the city of Bogota. This extraordinary formation seems to have been one mountain, but earthquakes and torrents have cut a wide breach and left the two peaks separated by a yawning chasm. The one called Guadalupe reaches a height of something like two thousand feet above the level of the city, and ten thousand feet above the sea. A small hermitage was built on the top of the mountain as far back as the year 1656, but this was destroyed by an earthquake in 1827. Forty years after, another church was commenced, as well as a monument. The whitewashed columns of these edifices may be seen from almost every part of the plain below—appearing like grim forts built to defend the city, which will, probably, never be in danger. The other height, called Monserrate, is separated from its neighbor only by a deep ravine. On the summit of this peak another church has been built, also whitewashed; this is somewhat lower than the other, and is approached by a winding track, in some parts almost perpendicular. A perpetual spring running out of the mountain has given rise to many legends, imputing miraculous power to its limpid waters. All that I saw about the water was that it appeared to me the purest and most sparkling I have ever seen. Another, and perhaps the most important of all the natural beauties of the surroundings of Bogota, is the celebrated waterfall, called El Tequendama, which is situated at a distance of about twelve miles from the city, in a south-westerly direction. The journey to the falls on horseback is very pleasant. The bridlepath runs through the fertile plantations and richly stocked pastures of the Colombian farmers. At a considerable distance the low, rumbling roar of the cataract may be heard, resembling distant thunder, and the nearer one approaches the falls the more beautiful the scenery. The river Funza, first coming from the higher Andes, at this altitude winds peacefully over a comparatively level plain, until it comes to a fearful abyss, over which the waters dash, to fall a distance of four hundred and fifty feet. The mighty precipices which wall in this wild rush of water rise to a height of about five hundred feet; they are beautiful with flowering shrubs, mosses, selaginellas, and orchids, which, in many instances, are suspended over the boiling waters, while large crowds of tropical birds move about amongst the suspended vegetation, lending a tint of colour and life to the grim boulders.

No visitor ever conies away disappointed; everyone leaves El Tequendama with an indelible impression of the grandeur of the spectacle, and some have even dared to call it a rival to the famous Niagara.

CHAPTER X

THIS MOST POPULAR ORCHID, *Odontoglossum crispum*, is found over a very wide range of country, extending on the north from the borders of the State of Cundinamarca to the frontier of Ecuador on the south. But although the district of the plant is so large, a little town called Pacho has always been the rendezvous of the collectors of *Odontoglossum crispum*, and it has already secured for itself fame in having produced the best varieties. This in many respects is right, as the flowers found in the range of mountains directly adjoining this village are, as a rule, round and full, of a fine form, and beautifully fringed, while on the more southern range the flowers are of the type known as "starry," or having the petals very much divided one from another. But many perfectly white flowers are found amongst the Pacho plants, and less of the highly blotched or spotted varieties so much sought after by connoisseurs; while, on the other hand, the starry varieties are, as a rule, mixed with thickly spotted flowers. Even while in Bogota I was on my way to these happy hunting grounds, and after a few days of looking around I started for Pacho. The distance is about fifty miles from Bogota, and the road by way of Cipaquira is very good. The traveller will pass on the way the house of a rich Colombian, Don Dematrio Parades. This is really a palace, where there is collected together one of the most beautiful displays of costly furniture and bric-a-brac to be found in Colombia.

From the town of Cipaquira the track runs directly over the salt-mine, and continues up to a height of about 8,000 feet to what is called the Paramo, then descends gradually to the town of Pacho. This occupies about two days, as most people find the journey sufficient to ride from Bogota to Cipaquira in one day. The appearance of the village of Pacho from the heights above is very picturesque: it is built in a valley, and just on the edge of some magnificent cattle estates; besides this, the houses are of fairly good construction. An Englishman of the name of Mr. Bunch was at one time owner of the extensive coal and iron mines here, and he has done much to improve the social condition of Pacho. The plant collector who arrives here very naturally thinks he will find the coveted *Odontoglossum* in the streets of the town; but, as a rule, the ardour of most of them is somewhat damped when they learn that a journey of three days must be made to the mountains before they can find a plant, if they would see it in its natural state. It took me very much longer. Within a circuit of fifty miles some plants are to be found, but especially in the direction of what is called San Cayetano, and to arrive here it is necessary to hire mules and provide provisions for three days' journey.

I left Pacho in the month of March, in the very height of the dry season. I was delighted to get away, as the facilities for living in Pacho are very bad, although always better than in the mountains. On the way from the town we passed the ironworks; these are very important for Colombia, there being only two mines worked in the whole country. There the labour is done by natives, superintended by a few Englishmen; they informed me that the neighbouring hills contain immense deposits of iron and coal, which are brought down on the backs of mules or in bullock-wagons. Before we reached the foot of the chain of mountains we had to cross the magnificent cattle estate, some miles in extent, which takes in the whole of the valley of Pacho. The land is very fertile, besides having an excellent climate and an abundance of water. We were not long in taking to the mountain track; the huge peak almost awed us as we looked up to it, towering above us to a height of 2,000 feet; and as we ascended the scenery took the most fantastic form. Immense boulders of incalculable height seemed to have been torn from their position and stood on edge. The stunted vegetation is crowded with large quantities of parasites of the family *Loranthus*, living on the sap of the tree which supports them. Many of these plants have lovely flowers, and one in particular, which was new to me, was covered with brilliant scarlet, waxy tubes about three inches long—these, of course, being utterly impossible to export in plant form, seeing that they derive their life from the sap of the tree on which they hang. All the birds I saw were birds of prey, probably on account of the shelter provided for them in the wild, impenetrable precipices which form the mountainside hawks, kites, and eagles wheeling around, poising themselves in mid-air, or swooping down with a fierce dart only to rise again bearing some careless squirrel or stray rabbit.

Occasionally a pair of condors might be seen, looking, even at that height, like giants amongst their neighbours. It was only after immense toil that I made half the ascent of the mountain; then I discovered that the boy who carried the provisions was nowhere to be seen. I had expected him to follow in the track; it was now after mid-day, and I had only passed one miserable hut, where, with difficulty, I had been able to procure a little refreshment. Anxiously looking for the boy at every turn, I kept on up the mountain until towards evening, being then about 8,000 feet above the level of the sea, when a thick mist came over the top of the mountain and rendered it almost impossible to keep to the track. I had heard that on the wide plain which forms the top of the mountain there was only one solitary hut, so to reach this with a tired mule was my determined aim. The conflicting tracks which intersect each other across the vast plain made progress doubly difficult. The first and most important thing in crossing this Paramo is to have an experienced guide; no European could possibly find his way alone, and even the best guides are often at a loss.

Finally we arrived at the hut, which had been dismantled by a recent hurricane, the fierce storm having taken away more than half the roof. The cold was intense—nearly freezing. The inhabitants of the hut were a family of the poorest Indians, and, although the only resources I could see were a few potatoes, their hospitality and good nature were scarcely credible. Having only brought the clothing with me which I used in the lowlands, I suffered very much from the cold. Almost the only vegetation found here is a large Edelweiss, which covers acres of the top of the Paramo; it is a plant growing about a yard high, the leaves, stems, and flowers being entirely enveloped in a woolly substance, probably to protect it from the cold. The other vegetation at this altitude is scarcely worth a name. Sometimes hail falls in large quantities, and nothing seems to give much result under cultivation except potatoes; of these the natives grow enough for their subsistence from one season to another.

My first night, passed at a height of twelve thousand feet above the level of the sea, was miserable enough, on account of the cold and the swarms of vermin. I was glad to get away early in the morning, although I had every reason to be grateful to the hospitable Indians, who, knowing that our provisions were lost on the way, gave us largely of their own little resources. In various parts of the Paramo I met with three birds which I was surprised to find: the first a tiny hummingbird,

Steganura Underwoodii, with the feet enveloped in tufts of white down, like miniature stockings, and two fine feathers in the tail longer than the rest, which finish by widening out at the end into a piece about the size of a silver threepence. The second was a hummingbird usually met with in the lower lands feeding on the flowers of the *Datura depressa*. Its bill seems to have grown with its necessity to reach the honey in the extremity of the long-tubed flowers; the bill of this extraordinary little mite is about two inches long and of the thickness of a darning-needle, being quite half an inch longer than the body. This variety of hummingbird is known to naturalists as the *Docimastes ensiferus*. The third was a bird about the size of a starling, gaudily colored, the upper part of the body black, the breast a brilliant scarlet, while a streak of rich blue ornaments each wing, and, as the bird flits across the plain with a springing motion, the alternate blue and scarlet make a pretty effect. This I judged to be the *Poecilothraupis lunulata*.

The mist had scarcely risen from the top of the mountains when we came in sight of the valley and range of mountains on the other side, where I expected to find *Odontoglossum odoratum*, knowing that this variety is found growing at a lower altitude than the *Odontoglossum crispum*, although they are both often found at a high altitude growing on the same tree. By evening we had made the descent of the tortuous path to the village of San Cayetano, most of the journey being made in a blinding rain. This village is situated on the very edge of the Odontoglossum forests. I expected to find someone here who would help me to get plants in the woods; but the people were too indolent for me to persuade them to work for wages, so I rested here for the night, and then kept on the journey further into the woods to a place called El Ortiz. I was told that here I could find people who would be willing to work in the mountains. We had scarcely entered the forest on this side of the mountain when I remarked a difference from anything I had seen before. The trees here were so grown together that they made a thick wood, while every branch and trunk was laden with a heavy coat of trailing lichen, perfectly dripping with water, so much so that, riding under them, our clothes were quickly wet through. In these natural reservoirs the *Odontoglossums* find their home at an altitude of from seven to eight thousand feet above the sea, with a temperature which often falls as low in the night as 500 Fahr., and I have never seen the thermometer rise above 590 Fahr. at midday.

Odontoglossum odoratum is most conspicuous as well for its heavy-branched spike of flowers as for its powerful smell, which fills the air until it becomes oppressive. The plants are almost hidden from sight in the trailing mass of lichen, and when they are not in flower they are difficult to find. I arrived at night at the hut called El Ortiz, after a toilsome ride, but the whole journey had been made through a wealth of orchids. Being informed by the natives that the *Odontoglossum crispum* had all been taken away from here, leaving only the *Odontoglossum odoratum*, I was obliged to continue my journey over the top of the mountain range, along a track which is too bad to describe, but, at the same time, the scenery is very beautiful.

After three days' journey, passing on the way a lovely valley rich with patches of sugarcane and maize, and also a small village called Buenavista, I struck into the forest, in the direction of the emerald mine. Here, at an altitude of about 8,500 feet above sea level, I found an abundance of plants, their magnificent spikes of flower looking doubly beautiful hanging from the branches of the trees, some high up out of reach of the native climbers, and others so low as to be easily pulled off by hand. My next consideration was to muster a company of natives sufficient to enable me to secure a quantity of the mountain treasures I had come so far to seek. These natives I encountered, to the number of about thirty, in the nearest village, called Maripi. Here, also, we found sufficient provisions for about a week; these were taken on the backs of mules to the edge of the forest, and then each man was supplied with his pack to carry through the forest to where we intended to make our camp, away on the edge of a mountain stream. The journey with the provisions took us two days, and on arriving at the site of our proposed camp we lost no time in constructing a rude hut, which served to shelter us for the first night, and which we eventually improved sufficiently to afford us protection for about a month. In those immense forests, where a few acres of clearing is considered a great benefit, and where clearings made, if not attended to, become forests again in three years, cutting down a few thousands of trees is no serious injury; so I provided my natives with axes and started them out on the work of cutting down all trees containing valuable orchids, and although for the first day or two they were very much given to mistake a clump of Bromeliaceae or Maxillaria for *Odontoglossum crispum*, they soon became adepts at plant collecting, and would bring to our camp several hundreds of plants each night, with occasionally a few *Odontoglossum odoratum* and *Odontoglos* mixed amongst them.

After about two months' work we had secured about ten thousand plants, cutting down to obtain these some four thousand trees, moving our camp as the plants became exhausted in the vicinity. Our next consideration was how to transport these plants to where sawn wood could be obtained. First, they had to be taken to the edge of the forest on men's backs; and even then we were five days' journey from the town of Pacho, where it is usual to make the boxes to pack the orchids in for shipment to England. We got over our difficulty by making about forty capacious baskets of thin sticks, cut in the forest. In these we packed all the plants, and carried them on the backs of bullocks to Pacho, where they were quickly placed in strong wooden cases, being still ten days' journey from the coast. From here mules are employed to travel with them to the banks of the Magdalena river, and from there the steamboats quickly transport them to the coastal town.

From the little village called Maripi, the celebrated emerald mines of Muzo may be reached by about two days' riding on mules. Probably very few people accustomed to see those lovely gems in their cut and mounted state have any idea of the difficulties to be undergone by those who would traverse this part of the Andes where the emerald mines are situated. The scenery is of the most extraordinary and beautiful to be found in Colombia, but in the two days' riding the traveller is obliged to pass through some of the most dangerous mountain passes, and over precipices where a false step would dash him and the mule to destruction. On arriving in the vicinity of the mines, the general appearance of the place would give one the idea that it was an extinct volcano, but the emeralds are found in the bottom of the crater. The piece of ground now being worked is surrounded by high mountains in a circle, giving it the form of a basin. All accounts of the exact date of the discovery of these mines seem to be somewhat faulty, although it is certain that they were known to the early Indians, for some emeralds have been found in the graves of Indians who must have been buried long before the conquest of the country by the Spaniards. The present system of working the mines has been employed about one hundred years. The mines are now the property of the Government of Colombia, who rent them to a company who employ five or six overseers and about four hundred native workmen. The means used for working the mines are very primitive, but they yield every year a very large amount of precious stones, which are immediately shipped to Europe. The bank of rock in which the precious crystals are found is more than one thousand feet high, formed of black shale veined with pyrites of iron. Very few emeralds are found in the black stone, but by cutting down the face of the immense precipice veins of white stone, calcite, a crystallized form of carbonate of lime, are uncovered in these veins. The emeralds are sometimes embedded and sometimes found in hollow cavities. The work of cutting down the side of the rock is done by the natives, their most powerful implement being a crowbar. A piece of rock about a yard wide is taken, the whole length of the mine, on the top; this is cut down a few yards, and then another level of the same is commenced again at the top, until the whole breast of the rock appears like a monster staircase, the broken rubbish being thrown over to the bottom of the precipice. On an opposite bank from where the emeralds are taken out, a stream of water is kept by means of sluices in a reservoir, and, as the sluices are opened every quarter of an hour, the water is allowed to rush down the rocks with great force, clearing away with the torrent all the broken stone thrown down by the miners since the last discharge.

The Colombian gentlemen who live here in charge of the workmen are among the most hospitable I have ever met, and whatever traveler chances to stray that way may be sure of a welcome from the emerald miners, who live in this mountain fastness sometimes for a whole year without making a journey to the adjoining towns. They informed me that they had explored the whole of the surrounding mountains for emeralds, and had found many places which yielded green stones, but none to produce the beautiful pure and dark green gems which are so prized, except the piece of rock now being worked, or, at least, not to produce enough to pay for the cost of working.

The next place of interest in the neighbourhood is the village called La Palma. This is two and a half days' journey on mules from the emerald mines in a north-westerly direction, being situated much lower than the *Odontoglossum crispum* district. The adjoining hills produce most splendid forms of *Cattleya Warscewiczii*. The ride is most enjoyable, the track lying through most beautiful scenery, especially along the banks of one small stream, where the trees are literally covered with

Cattleya labiata. When I passed that way a large number of them were in flower, presenting a sight of indescribable orchid beauty. Further along I met with a pretty delicate variety of *Comparettia* hung on the very tips of the branches of a kind of willow overhanging the water, so near that in the rainy season they must be submerged, while the majority of them must always be wet with spray.

The village of La Palma is one of the best of the old Spanish style, most curiously situated in a hollow of the tops of the mountains, which look like extinct volcanoes. The people are remarkably hospitable, and receive all travellers with the greatest kindness. Unhappily, the magnificent varieties of *Warscewiczii* have been cleared away from the neighbourhood long ago, and now, as in other parts, the orchid collector must take a journey of at least two days into the heart of the forest to get his plants, or send someone and wait three weeks in idleness and suspense in a monotonous village. The track into the forest is miserably bad, and to reach the plants is even dangerous; but those who have seen them in their forest home in all the glory of *Cattleya Warscewiczii* will admit with me that the sight is worth all the trouble of forest life. When I say that the sight of the plant in flower is very beautiful, orchid fanciers at home will imagine that large quantities are to be seen in bloom at once.

This is not generally the case with any class of orchids I have seen in their native woods; it is rare to see a tree with more than four or five plants, and these perhaps not all in flower at once; but in the good districts, before the plants were taken away so much, almost every tree and ledge of rock would have some one or more specimens in bloom, so that a large quantity might be seen in the course of one day. Near La Palma, but on higher, cooler ground, I found a few small plants of *Miltonia Phaloenopsis*, and in another locality quite a clump of *Oncidium Kramerianum*, as well as Chysis, Bolleas, and various Oncidiums. The vicinity of Muzo, near the emerald mine, is where I have found the largest quantity of the glorious Blue Butterfly (*Morpho Cypris*), some of them measuring seven inches across the wings, of a radiant blue that few artists' pencils can depict. Although *Cattleya Warscewiczii* is exported largely from La Palma, it is also found growing, mixed with *Cattleya Dowiana aurea*, in the State of Antioquia. I have collected *Odontoglossum Pescatorei* in the hills near to Ocaria, in the Department of Santander; but it would be wearisome to my readers to enumerate all that occurs in the tiresome ten days of riding over the Andes from the town of Bucaramanga to the *Pescatorei* grounds.

On the top of one of the high mountains on the way, near a village called Cachiri, at a height of 10,000 feet above sea level, I passed on the side of the track thousands of *Masdevallias*, chiefly of the *Harryana* variety. On another hill, two days' journey further along, but much lower, the trees are hung to crowding with the dainty little *Oncidium cucullatum*. Any future novice orchid hunter in search of *Odontoglossum Pescatorei*, will find it by leaving the town of Ocana, passing across the magnificent plains called La Savanna de la Cruz, and entering the chain of the Andes on the western side. Here, amongst the matted, moss-grown vegetation, *Pescatorei* is growing side by side with *Odontoglossum triumphans*, while the creeping rhizomes of *Odontoglossum coronarium* cover the roots of the same trees. I have seen the curious *Anguloa Clowesii* and the pretty *Ada aurantiaca* here as well, while in the cooler parts that choice little *Odontoglossum blandum* grows in profusion in a peculiar mist which reminds one of a continual Turkish bath. It is all very well to see this fastidious little orchid in its natural beauty, but it is quite another thing to succeed in bringing it home to England alive. Many of the plants die before they leave the coast, many more before they pass the West Indies; a few reach the Azores, and fewer still arrive in England safely.

CHAPTER XI

THE *CATTLEYA TRIANAE* HAS been found for years near the town of Ibague in the State of Tolima—a little more than one hundred miles from Bogota, in a southwesterly direction. This *Cattleya* is found under much the same circumstances as the others of its family, at an altitude of about four thousand feet above sea level. To reach it, it is necessary to ascend the river Magdalena for a considerable distance, and then land on the west bank. There is little of interest in the mule ride except the sight of the majestic snow-capped mountains, called the Paramo de Ruiz. These tower up to the height of sixteen thousand feet, with a glistening top of eternal snow, which makes them conspicuous at a great distance from many parts of the road. *Cattleya Trianae* is found over a wide area, but all the plants taken from these parts, as well as from Pacho, La Palma, etc., must be brought to a small town called Honda; this is the principal port of the Magdalena river, about six hundred miles from the sea. Swift running rapids prevent the larger steamboats going further up the river than Honda, but another line of boats has been built above the rapids. These vessels navigate the river for three hundred miles more to a place called Neiva. Hundreds of mules, carrying every imaginable class of produce, throng the road from Bogota to Honda. On arriving on the banks of the Magdalena everything in the way of cargo, animals, and human beings that would reach the town must embark in a curious kind of raft, attached to a strong chain stretching across the river; immediately the raft is loosened from the side, the force of the water carries it across the river, the pulley running along the supporting chain; this raft is worked from six o'clock in the morning until six in the evening, the small fee of twopence-halfpenny being charged for passing a horse and his rider, three-halfpence for a mule-load, and a penny for a foot passenger. A line of railway connects this place with the town of Honda, and runs to the part of the river where the steamboats land, called Yeguas, about four miles from Honda. At this point the mountains which wall in the valley of the Magdalena are very near to each other, and there seems to be no breeze which ever reaches the town; it is proverbially known all over the country as being very hot, and I have seldom seen the thermometer fall below 950 Fahr. in the shade.

It is a curiously built little town, with neither system nor design in the architecture. It was at one time large and important, but earthquakes have proved its ruin, and now the fine churches, convents, hospitals, and even a beautiful stone bridge, have all been destroyed. Travellers to the interior must inevitably pass this way, and everyone will find lodging houses and facilities for hiring mules, etc., to help him on his way to the capital. When I got on board the steamboat here to descend the Magdalena river, I practically said good-bye for the time being to four States of this magnificent country—Boyaca, Cundinamarca, El Cauca, and El Tolima. No pen or picture has or ever will be able to give more than a faint idea of the glories of this part of Colombia—of its riches in mines of emeralds and gold and silver; of its agricultural products of coffee, cocoa, and grain; of its trackless forests, with their exhaustless supply of timber and choice woods, its wealth of ornamental and medicinal plants, its bevies of gaudy-coloured birds and curious animals, its snowcapped mountains and boundless prairies where the Indians have always roamed with perfect freedom; or of its commercial cities, with their rich and cultivated inhabitants. Even the most stoical Englishman who has travelled here and seen its beauties cannot help but regret that so many thousand miles divide this paradise from our own little island.

The descent of the river Magdalena was made quickly and agreeably, and we very soon arrived at the port called Puerto Berrio. This is the port by which travelers reach the prosperous city of Medellin, one of the most important centres of the country, and the home of *Cattleya Dowiana aurea* and *Cattleya Warscewiczii*. Puerto Berrio has a special interest to all English orchid collectors. A rough cross of wood on the edge of the forest, on the higher bank of the river, marks the last resting place of Chesterton, the well-known orchid collector, who did such good service for the firm of James Veitch and Sons, long before the wholesale plunder and extermination of the plants brought about by modern collectors.

A small mountain town, called Frontino, has given, up to the present, all the *Miltonia vexillaria*, but the woods in the vicinity have become already pretty well cleared. I had heard much about the plants to be found between the river Opon and the river Carare: these are two rivers which together drain the southern part of the State of Santander, and the land lying between them is a narrow strip less than one hundred miles wide. I descended the river to a place called Barranca bermeja, with the object of getting a canoe to navigate the river Opon. This, I was told, would require at least six men, well-armed. The river is not navigable for more than fifty miles, and the distance is intercepted by fallen trees, while the forest between the two rivers is infested by hordes of hostile Indians. The first two days nothing extraordinary happened; the banks of the river were thick forest, and we saw no tracks of the Indians. Each night we camped on a sandbank. I saw no orchids, the land being too flat; but on the third day we passed many tracks of the Indians, and some abandoned huts.

About mid-day, as we suddenly made a curve in the river, a shower of arrows whistled past us and fell far ahead; they had been aimed too high and shot with too much force. In the direction the arrows came from we saw nothing, not even a rustling of the foliage. We fired several times into the bush, and proceeded more cautiously. My companions would have turned back, some of them becoming afraid, but an unconquerable curiosity possessed me to see what there was in the way of plants on the higher ground. It was evident that the Indians knew by this time, all along the river, of our ascent, and more than once I saw dusky forms creeping stealthily away from the banks as the canoe glided into sight. I had been informed that the Indians were very much scattered over the country, and although they maintain a deadly hatred against all civilised human beings, the fact of our ascending the river would not be sufficient to make them congregate in numbers, and the stragglers along the banks, although hostile in the highest degree, are cowardly and afraid of firearms.

On the fourth day, proceeding with the greatest difficulty on account of the fallen trees, we came to some three or four small sheds, with plantations of maize in front of them; a few animal skins were lying about, but every one of the inhabitants had taken to the woods. The very emptiness of the huts showed that their manner of life must be of the most primitive kind. However warlike they are towards outsiders, there are accounts that they live together in the greatest friendship and good faith. We left the huts very much as we found them, and proceeded up the river. I had seen several very pretty Oncidiums on the banks, and I had begun to hope we were clear of the Indians. On the night of the fourth day, we camped as usual on a sandbank, not being able to proceed further on account of the bad state of the river. Knowing that we were in the very middle of the Indian territory, where, if they chose, they could overpower us with numbers any moment, we passed the night somewhat nervously, with a very small fire, but with our rifles loaded, and while three slept the other three kept watch. Nothing happened to us that night, and early in the morning, after breakfasting, I started into the forest with four of the men, leaving the other two in ambush to watch the canoe, for fear the Indians should take away our only means of getting back to the Magdalena. I was delighted to find the trees on the rising ground from the banks of the river hung with fine clumps of *Miltonia vexillaria*, intermixed with *Oncidium Carthaginense* and several smaller orchids, and I was priding myself upon reaping a glorious harvest. But that night all my plans were destined to be crushed. Everybody was in good spirits at our evening meal, but we had scarcely finished and lighted our roll of tobacco when the twang of an arrow, as it whistled past my head, startled everyone to his feet.

In another moment one of our numbers was pierced with three of the deadly poisoned arrows, and mortally wounded. The moon was on the wane, and shed a miserable light for us to shoot by, while the savages could see us perfectly well by the light of our fire. Not a moment was lost in hiding ourselves behind the nearest trees, and we were scarcely placed when another shower of arrows showed us the position of the Indians. Seeing us retreat, they had advanced more into the open; at the same moment a blaze of fire poured out of five trusty rifles, and a terrible howl rose from the throats of the surprised and wounded Indians, who up to the present had not uttered a sound.

In a moment every mark for us to aim at had disappeared, but we fired another volley in the direction they had gone. For some time after, the rushing sound in the forest informed us that they were retreating and taking away their dead or wounded. I thought they would return, but my companions believed that the report of firearms was so little known to them that one encounter would be enough—and they proved right. As soon as day dawned we carefully reconnoitered in all directions. However, on that side we found nothing but the trail of the Indians and the pools of blood left by the victims of our bullets. I had been anxious to capture one of the Indians, so as to see what sort of people they really were, as up to the present I had caught nothing of them but the faintest glimpse; in this I was quite unexpectedly gratified. Two of the men were reconnoitering along the bank of the river near the canoe, when they came upon one of the Indians alone—probably a scout; he offered no resistance, but cowered on the ground as if to beg for mercy. I was surprised the two men had not shot him at first sight; but perhaps they were moved with pity, or were actuated by the same curiosity as myself—at any rate, I was as much surprised as the Indian when the two men brought him to me. He was a young man, apparently about twenty-two years of age, tall, and of a fine physical form; his skin was a rich bronze. I had heard that these Indians adorn themselves with feather head-dresses, but this one wore no ornaments, his only clothing being a small piece of grass-cloth tied around the loins. He was armed with the usual native bow, some arrows, and a lance. In the short time he was with us we were not successful in getting any communication whatever from him, even by signs, and he refused all food. I succeeded in getting a photograph of him; which operation I supposed he thought was to be the end of him, he appeared so frightened.

Apart from the vacant air of the untaught man of the woods, he had no savage look, and when left to himself in his own native haunts I should think he was good-natured. We took away his weapons, and then left him to return to his companions. In a moment he was off with a bound like a deer, and that was the last I saw of the Opon Indians. We quickly made a suitable resting place for our dead companion, and however loath we were to leave him there, we had no remedy. Loosing our canoe from its moorings, in less than two days the rapid stream landed us in the waters of the Magdalena; and for the future, however much I may covet the orchid gems of the headwaters of the Opon, they must remain there for my part until the last red man has disappeared from his territory.

CHAPTER XII

THE NORTHERN PART OF the chain of mountains between the River Cauca and the Magdalena had generally been considered rich in orchids, but up to the present few or none with a knowledge of plants had entered into the hills from the Magdalena side. The Cauca side of this chain of mountains is the home of the famous *Odontoglossum Harryanum*.

All the information I could rather about the eastern side of the range was that the Colombian merchants, Messrs. Lopez and Navarro, had sent an expedition two years before to explore these mountains in search of gold, at great risk and expense, employing many men. They had penetrated to the highest point in the northern part of the range—a high peak called La Tete de San Lucas, which is a barren rock on the top of a mountain something like eight thousand feet above sea level. I was determined to follow in their track, knowing that if I reached this altitude I should have passed through every zone of vegetation in the northern part of this range. I accordingly started in a canoe from a port on the banks of the Magdalena called Badillo. It was necessary to cross over to the western bank and follow an arm of the river, our object being to reach a small village called Simiti, situated at the foot of the mountains, but on the edge of a large lake called Lake Simiti. We followed the course of the river Magdalena for half a day, and then took a more westerly course, entering the mouth of a canal which drains the lake. This canal is very narrow, and in some parts only admits of two canoes passing each other; the vegetation on each side is like that of the rest of the valley of the Magdalena, being most luxuriant, and this part of the forest is full of game, especially the tapir and the capibara, while the branches of the trees are hung with egrets, large blue-and-white cranes, and kingfishers.

Another half-day brought us to Lake Simiti. It is a novel sight to emerge out of a narrow channel walled in on each side by thick forest into a magnificent sheet of water twelve miles long and seven miles broad, ornamented with several islands, each one covered with a wealth of tropical palms, while on one side of the lake the slopes of the Andes shelve down to the water's edge, and the towering peaks of the central range form the line of the horizon. Sunset here is a glorious sight; the coloured rays of light seem to rush down the mountainside and gild the waters of the lake, sometimes creatine a sort of mirage in which the forests of the Andes are represented with crowns of active volcanoes. About four hours' paddling in the canoe brought us to the village. This is at present but a miserable collection of mud huts. In the time of the Spaniards it was a rich and thickly populated town, but now all that remains of its former greatness are some two or three stone houses and two churches, which neither climate nor revolution has been able to affect.

One of them, which I photographed, is a good specimen of the early Spanish church in this country. History says the origin of the riches of this town were the goldmines of the vicinity, which yielded immense wealth to their Spanish owners; but when Spain lost her power in Colombia many of these mines were either lost or purposely filled up, and it is only lately that efforts are being made to discover these rich veins again. A large quantity of fine gold is annually washed out of various creeks and rivers by the natives, who use a flat wooden dish. The situation of this town is excellent, placed as it is on the edge of so fine a lake, which swarms with fish and myriads of waterfowl. The natives have no need for manual labor, as the lake and the forest provide them with all the necessaries of life. Here I was obliged to obtain men to carry provisions to the woods, as from here to the highest point reached by the expedition of Captain Lopez is nine days' journey on foot, and, except a few provisions to be obtained at the mines now being worked in the mountains, I was told that very little was to be had to eat. The first day's track ran through a kind of scrub and pastureland, which form the slopes of the hills, and along the side of the track there are sugar and coffee plantations. The second day was much the same, but the third day we had left all trace of habitation and struck into the thick forest, the principal living things I saw here being some wild turkeys and crowds of toucans. I suppose the track was made through the forest according to the caprice of the director of the expedition, for, to keep in the track, in about three miles of distance we were obliged to cross a serpentine kind of river nine times, always wading above our knees.

On the banks of this river I found many lovely specimens of *Oncidium Kramerianum*, but I did not stop to collect it, from a desire to know what there was on the higher grounds. At the end of the third day we had ascended something like three thousand feet, and on the morning of the fourth we arrived at the goldmines called La Concepcion, the property of Messrs. Lopez and Navarro, where the director, Mr. Thomas Smallfield, treated us with the greatest kindness. Although a miner's life in the wilds of the Andes must necessarily be full of privations, everyone seemed happy and contented. We rested here one day, and, after being furnished with a few necessaries by our friends the miners, we again started on the track. Two years had elapsed since the expedition passed that way, and then the road made was a mere trail. With the rank growth of vegetation in these climates this track had become entirely overgrown. Messrs. Lopez and Navarro believed that since the time of the Spaniards no one had set foot in these mountains but themselves, and, judging from the wildness of the rank, virgin forest, what they say must be correct.

Although I had one of the most expert guides who had taken part in the first expedition, we were continually losing ourselves, often having to branch out, turn back, or even climb trees, to find the direction of the track. The mountains on this side of the Magdalena differ from the orchid grounds in the eastern range in being thickly covered with immense timber trees of great height and thickness, while those on the eastern side are often only covered with a miserable scrub. It would be impossible to describe the peculiar undulations and deviations of the top of this range of mountains, not a quarter of a mile being level. First we would descend some thousand feet, letting ourselves down by creepers and shrubs as best we could, at the peril of our lives from a fall or from the deadly coral snakes which lurked on the shelves of the rocks; sometimes scrambling along; the bed of some mountain stream; then again we would climb with our packs of provisions another quarter of a mile almost perpendicularly, often on our hands and knees, always with the one object of reaching the highest point of the range, in order by so doing to pass through every variety of vegetation. It was important for us to camp each night where we found water—for instance, if we came to a stream about four o'clock in the afternoon we must not leave it, for fear darkness set in before we could find another. Two nights we were greatly inconvenienced by the side of the mountain being so steep that we were obliged to cut down a tree and lodge it lengthways against two others, then place our feet firmly against the horizontal tree, and so pass the night in a reclining position, the tree keeping us from sliding down the mountainside.

The journey from the mine to the top of San Lucas occupied six days of the hardest toil I have ever experienced, and when we reached the height our provisions were well-nigh exhausted; we had seen but few wild turkeys, the only living thing to be found in plenty being colonies of large black monkeys, which sat in the high trees grinning at us as we went past. The palms on some of the highest hills were torn up by the roots and split into shreds by the powerful black bears, which, however, did not trouble us. Of orchids there was a considerable variety, ranging from the Epidendrums of the arid plains to the Sobralias and Masdevallias of the cold regions; but the principal wealth of vegetation is in the variety of Anthuriums, tropical ferns, and other fine foliage plants. In one of the streams we almost lost ourselves in a perfect forest of Alocasias, some of these having a stem a foot in circumference and reaching a height of twenty feet. There were here also some very lovely plants I had not seen before of the family of the Gesneras, besides climbers, flowering shrubs, and Selaginellas.

The return journey to Simiti cost us seven days. Everyone arrived in good health, no one having suffered much apparently from our seventeen days' camping in the forest. I may say, for the encouragement of anyone who may choose to explore these mountains, whether in search of gold, or plants, or whatever it may be, that the natives here are the most trustworthy and the most enduring of fatigue of any I have met with. Those who went with me carried a heavy pack all day, climbing over the most inaccessible tracks, and at night preparing our camp, often under the greatest difficulty, the forest, as a rule, being dripping wet and the wood saturated. Our bread was procured by taking a bag of maize-meal with us, and every night one of the men made excellent cakes, enough to serve for next day's consumption. We had only one pot of any size, and it was a terrible blow to the community when the man who carried it fell down a precipice, his pack landing at the bottom first, and smashed our only means of making broth.

Everyone in the vicinity was loud in his praise of a part of the Magdalena adjoining what is known as the Santo Domingo river, so I determined to pay a visit to this district, and I can assure anyone coming after me that I was not disappointed. In Simiti the canoe is as indispensable to everyone as a horse is to the Gaucho, and the journey to the Santo Domingo, about fifty miles, is made by winding about amongst the various channels and small streams which cut up the immense savannas on the west bank of the Magdalena. The river Santo Domingo, after rushing down from the mountainside in the form of a noisy rivulet, suddenly gathers great force as it reaches the level land, and then, with the help of two small tributaries it receives, forms the only supply of four large lakes. It was near the borders of one of these lakes I took up my abode with a family of natives for a short time, with a view to exploring the forest on each side of the higher waters of the river, arid also with the object of securing some specimens of the curious waterfowl, etc., to be found around the edges of the lake.

The plains forming this side of the Magdalena are something like one hundred miles wide from the river to the foot of the chain of mountains. These plains are called by the natives La Savannas de San Luis. The land is very flat, mostly thick forest, sometimes intersected with swamp, in other parts with immense prairies, where the rank grass gives shelter to large herds of peccaries as well as to the tapir, jaguar, and puma. These plains are very scantily inhabited, the scattered natives living at a great distance from each other. Sometimes a family will have a ten-mile range of savanna for the few cattle they possess. The settlement where I lived was made up of three families, and in a southerly direction our nearest neighbors were at least seventy miles distant. The houses in which the natives live, although much superior to many Indian huts:, are still very temporary; in fact, they have no need of substantial dwellings, as they leave the low plains on the approach of the rainy season and migrate to higher grounds.

Animals of every kind become particularly daring here; they seem well aware they have little to fear from the indolent natives. The fat, unwieldy alligators, which elsewhere will generally shuffle into the water to hide themselves on the approach of anyone, here fight for the refuse food thrown into the river from the huts of the station; the jaguars and pumas, which have the reputation of being cowardly, are, on the contrary, a continual source of annoyance to the settlers, often making great havoc among the cattle, so much so that everything likely to serve as food for them must be driven into an enclosure made of stout poles for the night; the jaguar, or, as the natives call it, the tiger, often succeeds, however, in breaking through and taking away some dainty morsel in the form of a calf or a goat. The month of March is the time when the jaguars are most troublesome, and this happened to be the period at which I was on the savannas. In this month the turtles come out of the water during the night to deposit their eggs in the sandbanks, and the jaguars, actuated by some peculiar instinct, leave the more distant forests and live on the banks of the lakes, or in the vicinity. Although the turtles are both cunning and swift, hundreds of them annually fall a prey to the stealthy jaguar, which loses no time in scooping out every particle of flesh contained in its horny shell, but still without breaking it open; this they succeed in doing by inserting their powerful claws into the natural opening at each end of the shell. Every night while I lodged in the huts on the Santo Domingo we were disturbed by the roaring of the jaguars. Sometimes one would howl all night close to us; occasionally two and even three would call to each other from different parts of the lakeside or the forest. The male and female are easily distinguishable by their roar, in their natural state in the woods the call of the female being more prolonged and shrill than that of the male. I determined to try to rid ourselves of one or more of these unwelcome visitors. There were only two natives, however, in the settlement who were able to help me in a jaguar hunt, but we had plenty of dogs. The night before the proposed hunt we noticed well the situation of the beasts, as the natives know that the place where they howl at midnight is where they may be sought for at daybreak. We started away while it was dark, taking with us the best dogs of the settlement, and arrived on the edge of the lake where we expected to find our game just as the first streaks of dawn were appearing. It was evident by the signs of the dogs that the jaguars had been prowling around, but we were obliged to wait for more light. Very soon the deep footprints in the sand showed us in what direction to go, and half a mile of careful tracking around the edge of the lake brought us in sight of the jaguar. Then we dodged in amongst the bushes, keeping ourselves and the dogs as much under cover as possible, until by making a short cut we came down upon the beautiful animal at a distance of not more than twenty yards. It eyed us curiously for a moment, and then went off with a peculiar motion, like the action of a horse trotting, but we had the dogs in full cry at once. The jaguar went straight for the thick forest, but did not go far before the dogs came up with it, when it turned on its haunches and prepared to fight. It was wise for us to keep at a safe distance, to avoid the now infuriated animal springing upon us, and it was difficult to shoot for fear of hitting the dogs.

After ten minutes of desperate fighting the jaguar made a bound for the nearest tree, where it was out of the way of the dogs. I aimed a ball at the heart, but only broke the shoulder. However, this brought it again to the ground, and, mad with pain, it made a desperate spring at one of the natives, and came very near strangling him, bearing him to the ground with the force of the spring. It was a critical moment for my companion, and had the jaguar been still unwounded, instead of having a broken leg, it would probably have been the death of the native. While the mad beast was doing its best to clutch the neck of the prostrate Indian, I aimed a ball which struck the brain, and the sleek, beautiful animal rolled over motionless. It was a male, a fine specimen, measuring seven feet six inches from the nose to the tip of the tail. As we killed it in the thick jungle, where it was difficult to photograph, there was no alternative but to carry it on our shoulders to the edge of the lake, where we could get a good light. One of the Indians was so injured as to be unable to help in this operation, so I shouldered one end of the pole, being determined not to lose the chance of a picture. As soon as this had been satisfactorily accomplished, we were not long in taking off the skin, and this finished our adventure with the jaguar for this time, though by no means the only one.

Anyone looking at the adjoining picture may be puzzled to know how the photograph was taken under the circumstances. It was made with Messrs. Rouch's patent camera. I set the instrument in a position which I knew would produce the desired picture, and then instructed one of the natives to touch the spring which exposes the plate, this plate being carried away and developed at a more convenient time. An instance will illustrate how the turkey-buzzards and the vultures do their work in taking the place of scavengers. At the time we killed the jaguar not a bird was to be seen in the sky, but before we had taken off the skin at least a hundred vultures were wheeling overhead, and by evening a few scattered bones were all that remained of our game.

CHAPTER XIII

THE WATERFOWL WHICH CONGREGATE around the shores of these lakes in the months of March and April are to be found in such numbers that the description becomes almost incredible. I have seen, at a rough calculation, over four thousand in one flock, which extend themselves over a mile of the shallow water or sandbank. The most conspicuous amongst them are the immense storks, the *Mycteria Americana*, which stand five feet high, and look like soldiers with scarlet necks. It is very rarely the natives succeed in shooting one, but when they do quite a feast is made, as they consider the flesh very good food. Besides these, a smaller stork is to be seen in much larger numbers. Then come the blue herons, the large white cranes, the egrets, two or three varieties of bitterns, a crowd of large Muscovy ducks, a line of the awkward birds called "the Shag'," the snake-necked diver, and two kinds of small ducks, which to say are represented by hundreds would give but a poor idea of the cloud they make as they rise in the air. Although most of them are migratory, and few of them breed in this part, yet they are remarkably tame, having nothing to disturb them but an occasional passing canoe, and they remain stationary long enough for anyone to get a good sight of them, and even a photograph. Amongst the many varieties, the bird which seemed to me the most curious as well as the most strikingly beautiful is what is known as the Roseate Spoonbill (*Platalea ajaja*). It is about the size of a small goose, and it finds its food in the soft mud and sand, by digging up grubs and worms with its odd-shaped bill. The feathers are of a lovely rose-pink color, deepening into scarlet in the tail, and a band of the same colour runs across the wings. The peculiar satin-like texture greatly adds to their beauty. I succeeded in obtaining some five hundred specimens of birds of many species in this locality.

On account of the flatness of the land, orchids are somewhat scarce around the shores of the lakes; the most conspicuous of any note is the *Epidendrum atropurpureum album*, and as it flowers here, clinging to the bare trunks of the trees, it is a glorious sight. The spikes are long, crowded with flowers, and of the most distinct colors—not pale and washy, as is often the case in cultivation; sometimes it grows in clumps, which perfume the air for a distance around.

Although the Santo Domingo river is only navigable for about three days' journey in a canoe, it was necessary to fit up something like an expedition, so as to be able to explore more effectually the mountains beyond. My former privations in the San Lucas district had made me cautious enough not to start into an unknown country without provisions. But here we found later that we wanted very little more than the woods provided. In this locality there is such an abundance of fish and game that a tribe of Indians could support themselves for three months. Abandoned banana plantations are to be found at intervals along the banks of the rivers, still growing and bearing fruit with as much luxuriance as when the native owners cultivated them years before.

Further up the river we found orange trees laden with hundreds of luscious fruit, while the breadfruit (*Artocarpus incisa*) is a common timber-tree, growing in profusion all over the lower lands. This would provide wagonloads of its immense fruit, if there were a demand for it. Besides, in the season, when the mangoes are ripe, tons of the fruit are wasted. These, with the breadfruit, provide the means of living for herds of wild pigs and tapirs, which swarm the forest.

As we journeyed up the river through the floating Limnocharis and Pontederias, we came to another lake about six miles long. The thick forest coming right to the water's edge made it very beautiful. A company of natives had taken up fishing-quarters here for a week or two to lay in a stock of fish for the winter, and a description of their means of catching them may be interesting. The kind of fish most sought after, and which abounds the most, is the *Pimelodous tigrinus*, or catfish, which often attains a very large size. The natives go out in canoes, provided with about half-a-dozen harpoons, which are made in two sections. A sharp, barbed piece of iron is fixed to a piece of wood about two inches long, and this piece with the barb fits into a socket made in the end of a stout rod. The barbed piece is further attached to the long shaft by a stout cord. The native, as he moves about the lake or river in his canoe, makes a thumping noise to disturb the fish; this brings them to the top of the water, and their size, and the velocity with which they swim, make stream enough for the native who stands in the prow of the canoe to discern them; the moment he gets a good sight of the position of the fish he throws the harpoon with an aim that very rarely fails. The moment the fish is struck it darts off across the lake at a terrific speed. The barbed part of the harpoon detaches itself from the socket in the long shaft by the force of the water, but still remains connected with the canoe by the cord. The native then pursues the fish until it becomes exhausted, and sometimes the chase is most exciting. When the fish is so tired as to allow him to come up with it, it is knocked on the head with a cutlass and taken into the boat. Large quantities are annually caught by this means in the dry season, and cut into long strips to be salted for provisions for the time of floods. In the rainy season the only way that the natives can catch fish in the deep water is to shoot them with arrows when they rise to the surface to bask in the sun. This party of natives had already gathered together several hundred weight of fish, and as one company leaves the lakes it is succeeded by another, all through the dry season.

As we kept on up the river I saw several clumps of trees laden with the beautiful *Oncidium splendidum*, hung and trailing in the branches, looking quite a forest of orchids, their long spikes of bright yellow flowers appearing like a golden cloud in the tops of the tall timber-trees. A peculiar Schomburgkia I did not know was growing here, curious-looking enough with its pale-green flowers and long, mossy roots; the natives use the sap of the bulbs as gum for their cigars. The long rolls of tobacco which everyone smokes are first made from the leaves, and then the end is finished by sticking it with a little of the sap of this Schomburgkia. Most of the Indian huts have two or three old squaws who are adepts at this, and thus every hut has its own private tobacco manufactory. Apart from its utility in this respect, the plant has not merit enough to warrant it being brought to England, except as a botanical curiosity. Some of the trees which hung over the stream were laden with a pink-flowered Epidendrum, one of the *paniculatum* section, the branches being so heavy with the weight of the plants as to bend into the water.

I found a variety of bird here (*Trogan viridis*) I had not seen before in the lowlands; the breast of this species, instead of being scarlet or rose-colored like the most of its fellows, is a steel-blue, the back a shiny green, and the under part of the body yellow. I have found the same bird at an altitude of five thousand feet. Myself and my native helpers have had many adventures with snakes, from the delicate whipsnake to the mighty boa, which every living thing in the forest flees from and leaves master. An incident that happened here is curious enough to be worth mentioning. One evening I went for a stroll in the forest while the natives were preparing supper; some small birds known as the Red-winged Starling (*Leistes Guianensis*) were flitting about. I shot one, which fell from the tree still alive and fluttering; before I had time to catch it a large black-and-white snake, known to the natives as the "Hunter," sprang from an adjoining hollow tree, and, seizing the luck-less bird, was making off into the thicket at a quick pace. Fortunately, one barrel of my shotgun still remained loaded, and a snap-shot from this stopped its progress just as it was disappearing. This occurrence shows how much care is necessary in moving about in the forest, seeing how difficult it is to be aware of the presence of these venomous ene-mies.

In going up the river an event occurred, simple enough in itself, but which serves to illustrate how little the native is at a loss for re-sources under any circumstances. The canoe in which we travelled was a primitive structure made out of a hollowed tree, about thirty feet long, but very narrow. In this we travelled very swiftly where the water was smooth, but to begin to move about in it when it was in motion put us in danger of being thrown into the river. The man who had charge of the spoon-like paddle in the stern of the boat wanted to smoke, but had no tobacco; his companion in the prow had plenty. How to pass a cigar along the length of the craft while in motion appeared to me a difficult question. Not so to the native. His drinking cup, a calabash shell, was lying beside him; without a moment of reflection he placed one of the large rolls of native tobacco in the calabash and dropped it into the wa-ter; in another moment it had floated down stream and was alongside the native who sat in the stern; he coolly lifted the calabash out of the water, lighted his roll of tobacco, and went on his way rejoicing.

As we neared the higher waters of the river, navigation became more and more difficult, and before long we were obliged to tie up our canoe, make a kind of camp, and prepare to enter the forest on foot. The Santo Domingo river, in the part where it runs down the mountain-side, has always been famous for the quantity and purity of the gold found there. The natives have many legends about it as well as about the mountains of San Lucas. The story most in vogue before the expedition was sent by Captain Lopez was that the towering stone pinnacle seen from so great a distance was literally a deposit of gold, and that the higher part of the mountain was inhabited by some pigmy race of gold-diggers. Many of the men who accompanied the expedition were not a little surprised when they reached the pinnacle to find it nothing but a huge grey rock, and some were still more surprised when they were required to sign their names or put their mark to a document to certify to what they saw. The legend of the Santo Domingo is that in one of the higher parts of the river a vein of gold was known to the Spaniards, called by the name of "El Rosario," or the Rosary, and the natives believe to this day that their Spanish captors used to cut pure gold out of the rock with chisels. They also believe that at the time of the first revolution the vein was covered up purposely, and so lost. It is very rarely anyone penetrates into this forest, but when he does all the natives are on the alert, and the principal conversation is as to who shall find "El Rosario."

At this altitude food had become considerably more scarce than in the valley, and we were very pleased to be able to shoot an occasional wild turkey, the noble-looking bird known by the name of the Crested Curassow (*Crax alector*). I have found this species in nearly every part of Colombia, except on the high hills, feeding on fruit in the tops of the trees; it very rarely comes to the ground. I have shot male birds which weighed as much as twelve pounds. The flesh, when cooked, is tender, being nearly as good as that of the domesticated turkey. The beautiful little *Rodriguezia secunda* grows here in abundance, festooning the trees with wreaths of its pretty rose coloured flowers, mixed with *Comparettia Macroplectron* and a small variety of *Trichopilia*. The vegetation changes, as we ascend the mountainside, from the thick growth of the vegetable-ivory palm (*Phytelephas macrocarpa*) to the bamboo, and then again to the region of the tree-ferns.

To avoid the work of cutting a way through the forest we often kept along the mountain streams. One day, as I was wading up one of the streams at an altitude of about six thousand feet, I came upon that lovely little plant, the *Nertera depressa*, growing on the tops of stones about half-submerged in the cold water, but looking green and healthy, all covered with its bright red berries. I was the more surprised as I had never found it in any other locality, and was almost ignorant of its native country.

In the forests of Colombia, I have met with four species of toucans at various altitudes. Here we were besieged by crowds of the large black variety, with a golden-yellow patch on the breast and the usual awkward bill. I had no difficulty in securing a few as specimens.

We very soon reached the height of the Cattleya grounds; but for anyone to get a good collection here it is necessary to camp in the forest and work three weeks with a good company of men. The plants are most difficult to carry through the woods to the canoes, and they must be taken by way of Simiti, where it is easy to get wood to make boxes; but when they are made another difficulty presents itself. The canoes used here are small, and not capable of containing more than half-a-dozen plant-boxes each, and then there is a great danger of having them thrown into the river by the least carelessness on the part of the boat-men.

In making the descent of the Santo Domingo river we came upon a colony of Weaver Birds (*Cassicus periscus*). These attractive little birds live in companies sometimes amounting to several hundreds, and they generally choose a high tree quite isolated, and there hang their peculiarly made nests to the extremities of the branches which project most from the trunk in a horizontal position. I have met with several species, all apparently of the same habits. The nests of the one I saw on the Santo Domingo were perfect works of art, about two feet long, made of the fine, dry stems of climbing plants, and woven together in a way that would make it difficult to believe they were the work of so small an architect. They are narrow at the top and wide at the bottom, looking like huge stockings floating in the wind; the wide, bulging part at the bottom is occupied by a nice bed made of the soft seed covering of the Asclepias, and in this the female lays two tiny spotted eggs; an aperture is left in the top of the nest just large enough for the occupants to pass in and out, and at the same time to look like a trap to snakes and other enemies. The cleverness with which they use their needle-like beaks in working the twigs, and the agility they display in running in and out of their sack-like home, are perfectly wonderful. The male bird is of a shiny black, with a spot of rich orange on the back, the female being scarcely so attractive. They seem by their gentle habits to be birds which could be easily tamed, and if it were possible to keep them in confinement they would be universal favorites.

I left this part of the country by way of the village of Simiti. As the canoes glided dreamily across the beautiful lake, the sun, just rising over the tops of the distant mountains, threw a soft rosy tint on the waters, and this, with the picturesque islands covered with dark green waving palms, made up a scene which is as indelible in the memory of the traveler as it is indescribable to the reader.

After leaving Lake Simiti the canoes followed a channel into the river Magdalena, where they occupied nearly a whole day in going round the point of an immense island in order to arrive at the station, Bodega Central, where passengers must wait to meet the steamboats going down the river to the coast. I had four whole days to spend here before one would come down. A pair of jaguars had been committing nightly depredations on the cattle of the settlement, taking away half-grown cows, calves, pigs, and even coming into the streets of the village and making a meal of one of the dogs. So, to pass the time while waiting for the boat, I determined to try a system employed by the Indians to take them—that is, to tie a calf or a young pig to a stake in some open place in the forest and wait in ambush. The nights were beautifully light, the moon being full, and with clear air in this climate it is possible to see well by moonlight; so, accordingly, I fixed upon a situation about half a mile from the village, and tied a pig to a stake. I then climbed into a luxuriant mango tree, preparing my gun with a good charge of ball to be ready for any visitor. Just at this season the luscious mangoes are ripe, and as they ripen they become detached and fall to the ground. Every night a large quantity fall, providing food for the peccaries, tapirs, and the domesticated pigs of the settlement, which come through the night to feed upon them. The first night nothing came near me but a few of these animals. About midnight the jaguar took a pig away from one of the huts. I could hear it squeal as it was being borne into the forest. The second night I changed my situation; this time a fox and several tiger-cats came close to me, but the jaguar did not appear. The nights were lovely; I wish it were possible to describe a moonlight night in a tropical forest, but this must be experienced to be understood. The third night several smaller animals visited me, and a splendid jaguar crossed the open space where I was hidden. I could see the beautiful spots on the skin; but I did not fire, in hopes that the animal would come nearer to spring upon the bait. In this I was disappointed—no doubt, the quick sense of smell which the jaguar possesses warned him there was danger—and I was obliged to take the boat down the river the next day without being able to add another jaguar's skin to the nine I had already.

On the river-steamboats it is very difficult to carry orchids safely, on account of the space for cargo being in such close proximity to the boilers, and the heat so intense. On arriving at Barranquilla many fine specimens in my collection were lost. In this I am not alone, as every traveller has found that however well his plants are packed, and however carefully looked after, many much-prized specimens, that have cost so much labour and hardship to obtain, have to be thrown overboard and left to finish rotting in the muddy waters of the Magdalena. I was fortunate in securing a passage at once by the Royal Mail Company's steamship *Essequibo*. On the journey from Barranquilla to the port there was the usual delay and annoyance, the only difference being that I was not able to land at a place called Savanilla, or Salgar. The shifting sands of the Magdalena have filled this up so that vessels cannot come near, and another port has been made, with a few sheds and a temporary stage, further along the coast, and this bears the name of Puerto Colombia. It is said that a contract has been entered into with an English company to supply the material and build a substantial pier, etc. Let us hope that it will be completed before any of my readers have to land there.

CHAPTER XIV

THE *ESSEQUIBO* WAS NOT long in weighing anchor, keeping along the coast, bound for the Port of Carthagena. As we left in the evening, and the journey is only of a few hours, we found ourselves in the morning opposite this curious, old, historic port and city. Its substantial towers and immense walls, with their picturesque surroundings of mountains and forts, give it a more imposing appearance from the sea than any other place I have seen in the north of South America. History is so full of accounts of the sieges and battles, the persecution and bloodshed, enacted here in the time of the Spaniards and the pirate buccaneers that it is almost superfluous for me to recount them. Before these wars the entrance to the city for ships was made through either of two beautiful bays, both of which were excellent harbours. One of these is called Boca Chica, and the other Boca Grande; but as the inhabitants were being continually robbed and murdered by the buccaneers, who came in galleys and entered by way of the smaller port, Boca Chica, the colonists determined to stop their inroads by filling up the entrance to the harbour. This they actually succeeded in doing by means of large stones, with an amount of labour which makes the story almost incredible, but at the same time destroying their best port. This not being sufficient, Philip II. of Spain caused a wall to be built around the city at a cost of fifty-nine millions of gold dollars. It is so wide that forty horses can walk abreast on the top of it. However that may be, neither time nor weapons have been able to damage it much; it still stands, a fine old monument and a triumph of masonry. History says that none of these means were of any use in protecting the people. The bands of robbers continued to pillage the town and take away tons of gold and silver, which annually came from the rich mines in the interior to be shipped to Spain—each invasion witnessing the same scenes of cruelty and carnage.

The vessels lay at some distance from the quay, but a landing was easily effected by means of any of the small boats in waiting, the water of the bay being generally as smooth as glass. As the time spent here by the Royal Mail ships is very short, we were soon on shore to see as much of the place as the time would allow. The houses are most curious, looking like a city of forts. Many of them are spacious, and even palatial; the massive stone walls are at least four feet thick, and the spaces for the windows fitted with strong iron bars. They are built round a square, open court, after the Moorish style, the heavy doors, which form the only entrance, reminding one of the old English portcullis; and though many of them are half-ruined and deserted, they give an idea of what Carthagena must have been in its glory. I visited what is called the Inquisition Building, the only one of the kind left in Colombia. For nearly sixty years after the then despotic power of the Romish Church had been overthrown it stood empty; it is now the residence of a rich citizen, and although it was once fitted with instruments of torture, and prison-cells where hundreds died a miserable death, very little remains in the immense building to prove what deeds of horror were enacted within its walls.

There are two cathedrals, one of the time of the early settlers, and one modern—both beautiful specimens of architecture, adorned with the usual extravagant decorations of high-class Roman Catholic places of worship. In the oldest of these is located the famous marble pulpit. The story told about it by the people reads more like romance than sober fact. The tale has it that one of the Popes, who wanted to present the faithful at Carthagena with something to perpetuate his memory, and at the same time to adorn the magnificent cathedral, ordered the pulpit to be designed and sculptured by the very best artists of the day in Rome. When the work was finished, it was placed on board a Spanish galley and despatched to Carthagena. In the course of the voyage the vessel was captured by pirates, and the boxes containing the pulpit, upon being broken open and found to be of no value as plunder, were thrown overboard, but, by the interposition of the Virgin, none of the pieces sank. The English pirates, becoming alarmed at the miracle of the heavy marble floating on the water, fled from the ship, leaving their booty. The Spanish sailors got the precious cargo aboard their vessel again with great difficulty, and continued on their way; but before they reached Carthagena they encountered a second lot of pirates, who plundered them of all their valuables and burned the ship. However, the saints still preserved the pulpit; for as the vessel and the remainder of the cargo were destroyed, the carved marble floated away upon the surface of the water, and, being guided by an invisible hand, went ashore on the beach outside the city to which it was destined. There it lay for many years unknown and unnoticed. Finally, it was discovered by a party of explorers, who, recognize the value of the carvings, took it aboard their ship en route for Spain, intending to sell it when they reached home. But the saints still kept their eyes upon the Pope's offering, and sent the vessel such bad weather that the captain was compelled to put into the port of Carthagena for repairs. There he told the story of the marble found upon the beach, and it reached the ears of the archbishop. His Grace sent for the captain and informed him that the pulpit was intended for the decoration of the cathedral, and related the story of its construction and disappearance; the captain did not seem inclined to believe the story, but offered to sell the marble, and would not leave it otherwise.

Having repaired the damage done by the storm, the captain started for Europe; but he was scarcely out of the harbour when a most frightful gale struck him and wrecked his vessel, which went to the bottom with all on board; but the pulpit, the subject of so many divine interpositions, rose from the wreck, and one morning came floating into the harbour of Carthagena, where it was taken in charge by the archbishop and placed in the cathedral for which it was intended, and where it now stands. The story may be taken for what it is worth; but one thing is undeniable—the quality and variety of the marble used, and the richness and beauty of the sculpture, must give it a place amongst the first objects of art in the world.

Besides the many rare and costly altarpieces and carvings to be seen here, there is one object so curious as to be worthy of a special remark. This is the preserved body of a saint. I do not remember whether any name is affixed to the coffin; but the story says he was a great favorite with the people of Carthagena, and when he died they asked as a favor that the Pope would allow his body to be embalmed and sent to their church, and there it is to this day. The saint is placed in a glass coffin, which stands upon a marble pedestal. The body is somewhat shriveled, but not, as one noted writer has irreverently put it, like jerked beef. Some have described the body as a hideous spectacle, but I saw nothing repulsive about it. The saint appears to have been a man of middle height, and as the body lies there it is clad in a coat of ancient mail, with a sword and other accoutrements.

After leaving the cathedral, I wandered about the old city, admiring the many beautiful statues and the curious masonry, until the Essequibo was ready to sail. Formerly the city was connected with the river Magdalena by a ship canal; this still exists, but it is very much filled up by the forest encroachment, and in the dry season it is almost impassable. In leaving the harbour again we got another sight of the wonderful fortifications. The massive walls of the city are to all appearances impregnable, and the ancient passages or covered ways leading outward to the foot of the adjacent mountains are still visible; while the sides of the magnificent harbour are studded with grim forts, which, though now unused for more than half a century, seem almost as good as new.

Our next port of call was Colon, so famous for being the entrance to the Panama Canal from the Atlantic side. This is only a few hours' sail from Carthagena, along the rugged Colombian coast, passing on the way the Indian territory and the Gulf of Darien. The scenery is wild and beautiful, and the harbour of Colon is considerably more attractive from the sea than on shore. Although there is the advantage, if it may be called one, of the ship lying alongside the wharf, yet the change from the romantic surroundings of Carthagena to the more modern filth and disorder of Colon is anything but agreeable. With the colossal project of uniting the two great oceans came what appears to be the scum of all nations, if one may form an opinion by looking into the American bars, Chinese drinking-shops, and gambling-hells, which seem to leave no room for any settled comfort or the formation of a regular community

The houses had nearly all been built of wood, in the most matchbox style it is possible to imagine, before the last fire. The ground-floor was a kind of open shed which supported several flats, and each of these flats was divided into honeycomb-like sections, each section occupied by a family or part of one. The number of people and the numerous nationalities at one time crowded into these small rooms is almost incredible. Such a strange and cosmopolitan company as is to be seen in the streets of Colon is rarely to be met with. A large percentage of the laborers are negroes; there are also hordes of Chinese, a few Arabs and coolies, a company of Frenchmen, a few English and Americans, Spaniards, Cubans, and Colombians; and occasionally a band of half-civilized Indians from the interior may be seen moving about amongst the stores, making purchases, always in company. Here everything has an air of neglected dissipation, and the motto of Jew and Gentile seems to be either to kill themselves with rum or make a fortune.

The place has suffered very much from fire, having been twice almost entirely swept away. The part of the town adjoining the entrance to the canal is called the Quartier Francais. An avenue of coconut palms, which were planted some years ago, now form a pretty and an agreeable shade. In this neighborhood are situated the houses of the Frenchmen employed in directing the work of the canal; they are neat little cottages, built of wood, and provided with a verandah where the new imports from Paris can swine in their hammocks and contemplate the ocean or sunny France on the distant other side. Just at the point of the entrance to the canal two spacious wooden houses have been built for the use of the famous engineer, M. Ferdinand de Lesseps, while in front of these, on the very edge of the water, is placed a beautiful bronze statue of Christopher Columbus protecting an Indian. This was presented to Colon by the Empress Eugenie in the time of her power. Although at the time we passed Colon the actual work of the canal was suspended for want of capital, the seven miles already open for traffic were busy with boats and small steamers, while the sides were stocked with machinery and workshops. As the Royal Mail ships lie here three or four days, travelers have time to take the train across the isthmus to the town of Panama, the Pacific entrance to the canal. In the journey a good idea may be formed of the work of excavating which is being done; and the scenery is good, while the town is very much more commodious than Colon.

At Colon we were obliged to transship to the homeward-bound mail, the *S.S. Tagus*, everyone being sorry to leave the excellent and kindly captain of the *Essequibo*, Captain Buckley. The *Tagus* was soon on its way to Jamaica. The mosquitoes and the bad climate, together with the filth and disorder of Colon, made everyone glad that the stay here was not longer. So much has been written from time to time about the beautiful island of Jamaica that there is no need here for me to do more than merely mention the port. Sailing along the coast, we soon come in sight of the shallows and the jutting projection with the fortifications called Port Royal. As the waves dash up on the sandy beach the strong light of this climate gives the water a most lovely transparent blue colour which is seldom seen in more northern latitudes. Kingston

Harbour is one of the most important in the West Indian Islands, and is always well filled with ships of every kind and nation, from the magnificent modern man-of-war and merchant ship to the tiny sail-boat that trades along the coast with fruit. The appearance of this island from the sea is very much improved by a range of hills which extends the whole length of the interior. These are very rightly called the Blue Mountains, as they are mostly covered with a thin mist which looks from the sea like a pale-blue gauze thrown over them, changing with the rays of the sun to the most fantastic colours. As the ships lie alongside the quay, passengers are at liberty to stroll on shore to visit the places of interest in the town of Kingston. Some take apartments in hotels to avoid the uncomfortable heat of the ship, others make excursions to various parts of the island. The town itself, although full of business activity, is hot and dusty. The most favourite resorts in the country are the lovely model Botanical Gardens, which occupy one of the best situations half a day's journey up the Blue Mountains, and the military station, which lies far up the side of the mountain, where the air is cool and pure. Last year the Exhibition of manufactured goods and products of the islands was a great attraction to Kingston.

Tram-cars run to one of the suburbs called Constant Spring, about an hour's ride from Kingston, passing on the way many pretty villas, in which the wealthy inhabitants of the town take refuge from business. A commodious hotel has been built at this place, offering every convenience for visitors. The beautiful park, called the Victoria Park, is rich with a wealth of tropical plants which every foreigner covets; the keeping and arrangement of the plants are carried out with the greatest crood taste. Although a large part of the island is mountainous and uncultivated, there are many fine sugar estates, and the growing of sugar-cane and making of sugar and rum occupy most of the labour of the island. Every variety of tropical fruit is in lavish abundance, especially pineapples, many of which find their way to the London market. Some of the Oncidiums grow in profusion in the climate of Jamaica. Many of the cottages have quite a quantity of plants, which flower very freely and look extremely pretty. Although the negroes are generally averse to hard work, it would probably be difficult to find a more peaceable, law-abiding community than the coloured population of the island of Jamaica. In the country their tiny hovels are little removed from sheds, often miserably neglected, but in the towns many of the houses are furnished with the greatest care and comfort The inhabitants of the outlying hamlets are occupied largely in producing fruit for the market of Kingston, and in the season of the ripening of the mangoes they seem, like the South American Indians, to subsist almost entirely on this fruit; while the Papaw (Carica papaya) and the Avocado pear (Laurus Per sea) form the dessert.

Although many of the streets of Kingston are narrow and badly kept, the houses are built so as to ensure the greatest comfort to the inhabitants of a hot climate. The large, airy saloons, which are often on the second floor, are formed of partitions of latticework, which exclude largely the dust and insects, and at the same time admit of a free circulation of air, and so keep the dwellings as cool and agreeable as possible.

As we had been four days delayed at Colon, and two more at Jamaica, anyone having a valuable cargo of plants from the cool regions of the Andes would naturally be uneasy about their safety in. the roasting heat of these ports, so I was only too pleased when we steamed past Port Royal on our way to the island of Haiti. The *Tagus* coasted along the island, and then put into the harbour of Jacmel, only to deliver mails and passengers, which occupies a very short time. The sight from the sea is very picturesque, but no one lands here excepting those who have business, and, however beautiful this island may be, very little seems to be known about it to the outside world. For my part, after the journey thus described, I was in no mood to undertake the task. The *Tagus* put into the harbour of Bridgetown, Barbados, just by way of a call to see our friends, and then betook herself to the eleven days' journey across the Atlantic. As a rule, the large company of Colonials who come on board at the various islands are not the best of sailors, and there is the usual period of seasickness to get over; but long before we reached the Azores everyone was on deck enjoying the beautiful passage, which continued until we reached the Lizard. Finally we reached the lovely harbour of Plymouth, where many an exile who had lived a stranger in a strange land was glad enough to again set foot on Old England.

THE END

Printed in the USA
CPSIA information can be obtained
at www.ICGtesting.com
LVHW050439310723
753861LV00011B/654